T0291320

Economics, Education and Youth Entrepreneurship

The aim of this book is to justify the importance of economic knowledge for every human being in a country with an economic system based on the market mechanism, and to explain and debunk the myths and stereotypes related to economic education and its effectiveness, particularly among young people.

The book offers a comparative analysis of the economic education of young people in Poland and throughout the world. It examines the historical emergence of economies and economic thinking and decision-making as well as the different philosophies and educational systems in the EU and the USA. It thoroughly investigates the economic knowledge of Polish youth via an annual study, which the authors have conducted since 2012.

The book outlines both the formal and informal methods of economic education, from education programs in general secondary schools and economic technical schools, as well as in vocational schools, and also examines school Business Incubators. It concludes with a summary, reviewing the implementation of research goals and issues and outlining directions for future research.

The authors break down complex topics and provide readers with a base knowledge of economics at the micro and macro levels. The book will serve as a useful and practical guide for students and researchers, as well as policymakers concerned with rethinking the education system. Additionally, it will be a helpful resource for those wanting to acquire the knowledge needed to conduct a business, as the authors maintain that entrepreneurship can be learned.

Marian Noga, PhD, is Professor of Economics and Head of the Business Cooperation Institute of WSB University in Wroclaw, Poland. He is also former Senator of the Republic of Poland, former Member of the Monetary Policy Council of Poland and former Rector of Wroclaw University of Economics, Poland.

Andrzej Brzeziński, PhD, is Associate Professor of Częstochowa University of Technology, Faculty of Management and an associate of Wroclaw University of Economics and Business, Poland. He has developed and implements the nationwide educational and research project The Entrepreneurship and Management Olympiad (currently VIII edition), which is ranked among the best economic contests in Poland.

Routledge Focus on Economics and Finance

The fields of economics are constantly expanding and evolving. This growth presents challenges for readers trying to keep up with the latest important insights. Routledge Focus on Economics and Finance presents short books on the latest big topics, linking in with the most cutting-edge economics research.

Individually, each title in the series provides coverage of a key academic topic, whilst collectively the series forms a comprehensive collection across the whole spectrum of economics.

Foreign Exchange Rates
A Research Overview of the Latest Prediction Techniques
Arif Orçun Söylemez

Islamic Economics and COVID-19
The Economic, Social and Scientific Consequences of
a Global Pandemic
Masudul Alam Choudhury

The Economics of Intellectual Property and Openness
The Tragedy of Intangible Abundance
Bartłomiej Biga

Economics, Education and Youth Entrepreneurship
International Perspectives
Marian Noga and Andrzej Brzeziński

For more information about this series, please visit www.routledge.com/
Routledge-Focus-on-Economics-and-Finance/book-series/RFEF

Economics, Education and Youth Entrepreneurship

International Perspectives

Marian Noga and
Andrzej Brzeziński

Routledge
Taylor & Francis Group

LONDON AND NEW YORK

First published 2022
by Routledge
2 Park Square, Milton Park, Abingdon, Oxon OX14 4RN

and by Routledge
605 Third Avenue, New York, NY 10158

Routledge is an imprint of the Taylor & Francis Group, an informa business

© 2022 Marian Noga and Andrzej Brzeziński

The right of Marian Noga and Andrzej Brzeziński to be identified as authors of this work has been asserted by them in accordance with sections 77 and 78 of the Copyright, Designs and Patents Act 1988.

All rights reserved. No part of this book may be reprinted or reproduced or utilised in any form or by any electronic, mechanical, or other means, now known or hereafter invented, including photocopying and recording, or in any information storage or retrieval system, without permission in writing from the publishers.

Trademark notice: Product or corporate names may be trademarks or registered trademarks, and are used only for identification and explanation without intent to infringe.

British Library Cataloguing-in-Publication Data
A catalogue record for this book is available from the British Library

Library of Congress Cataloging-in-Publication Data
Names: Noga, Marian, author. | Brzeziński, Andrzej Maciej, author.
Title: Economics, education and youth entrepreneurship : international perspectives / Marian Noga, Andrzej Brzeziński.
Description: Abingdon, Oxon ; New York, NY : Routledge, 2022. | Series: Routledge focus on economics and finance | Includes bibliographical references and index.
Identifiers: LCCN 2021017812 (print) | LCCN 2021017813 (ebook)
Subjects: LCSH: Economics—Study and teaching—Poland. | Youth—Poland. | Entrepreneurship—Poland.
Classification: LCC HB74.9.P7 N64 2022 (print) | LCC HB74.9.P7 (ebook) | DDC 330.09438—dc23
LC record available at https://lccn.loc.gov/2021017812
LC ebook record available at https://lccn.loc.gov/2021017813

ISBN: 978-1-032-07321-7 (hbk)
ISBN: 978-1-032-07324-8 (pbk)
ISBN: 978-1-003-20644-6 (ebk)

DOI: 10.4324/9781003206446

Typeset in Times New Roman
by codeMantra

Contents

Figures

Tables

Introduction

One must live long to learn or It is never late to learn – this is a commonly known saying all over the world. The market economy, which has been developing for almost 300 years in various variants, has shown that satisfying our various innate and acquired needs requires a certain economic knowledge. Most often, people acquired this knowledge in contacts with other people, in and outside the market. Nowadays, we would define this form of learning as *learning by doing*. This knowledge was sufficient only when the state played the role of a "night watchman" and did not interfere in economic processes. But the need to ensure social and economic order made the state an economic entity that made macroeconomic regulatory decisions, which is referred to as economic interventionism. State interference in economic processes is usually carried out by means of fiscal and monetary policy, which means that the microeconomic knowledge gained by people in their actions was no longer sufficient. Fiscal policy and, even more so, monetary policy are quite complex and require macroeconomic knowledge. Moreover, households operated not only within one national economy but also in the entire system of national economies, in groupings of states such as the European Union, which was called the processes of globalisation.

These facts made it necessary to conduct economic education in such a way that people could freely work, study and meet their needs. The market economy has determined the basic principle of the functioning of modern society: every person should be a conscious consumer, employee and entrepreneur if they want to independently implement their idea for a business for applying entrepreneurship in economic practice. Of course, the first steps of economic education were spontaneous and poorly coordinated by the state. Usually, people were educated economically after high school graduation and after studies, through training, courses, postgraduate studies at various

DOI: 10.4324/9781003206446

levels, then economic education was introduced in studies, and finally, it was realised that economic education should be started already in secondary school. This was due to various reasons:

- People after high school graduation started families and needed economic knowledge immediately;
- In households, economic decisions were made not only by adults but also by children – it was a characteristic group way of making decisions, which is used today, for example, in corporations;
- Economic awareness was necessary at the stage of making decisions by a teenager, whose pocket money was, for example, PLN 100 and he could buy an album of his favourite band for PLN 40 or go to a concert of this band, for which the ticket cost PLN 75. He could not acquire both of these goods, but he found that the economic cost of the album = PLN 115 [actual cost of the album PLN 40 + alternative cost PLN 75] and the economic cost of the concert also = PLN 115 [actual cost of the concert PLN 75 + alternative cost PLN 40]. A young Pole knows where Argentina, Japan and Egypt are located, but he does not know where the price of chewing gum comes from, as a young English, American or French does.

These events made us decide to write a monograph devoted to the economic education of Polish youth because we have only been getting to know the nature of the market economy in Poland since 1989, and young Germans, English, Americans, Japanese and French have been getting to know these features for 300 years.

The aim of our monograph is to justify the importance of economic knowledge for the life of every human being in a country with an economic system based on the market mechanism and to explain and debunk myths and stereotypes related to economic education and their effectiveness.

The European Commission in its communication of December 18, 2007 stated that "Consumers should learn about economic and financial matters as soon as possible". On the other hand, the OECD, the organisation of the most developed countries in the world to which Poland belongs, stated in 2005 that "The government and other stakeholders should promote objective, ethical and coordinated financial knowledge". It was a reaction to the promotional activities of various financial pyramids, near banks, institutions granting loans at usurious interest rates in a dishonest way. A young person is exposed to this type of unfair practices, and economic knowledge is essential for creating a socio-economic order.

In the monograph, we will verify the following scientific hypothesis:

> Economic education of Polish youth cannot be left in the hands of family and household, but it must be institutional and international, and it should be coordinated and controlled by state bodies using standard and non-standard instruments.

The monograph consists of three chapters, the first two are theoretical and the third is empirical.

The first chapter, entitled "The need to disseminate economic knowledge of young people in the modern world", is devoted primarily to the comparative analysis of economic education of young people in Poland and in the world. We show here how the economy came into being, what the nature of economic laws is and how they should be used in the processes of management and making economic decisions.

Chapter 2 "Formal and informal methods of economic education of young people in Poland and in the world" is devoted to economic education programs in general secondary schools and economic technical schools, as well as in vocational schools, and finally, the topic of school Business Incubators. It is in this chapter that we present the mistakes in economic education in Poland – in the light such education in the world – and show what myths and stereotypes are about when assessing the effectiveness of economic knowledge in Poland.

Chapter 3 entitled "Economic knowledge of students in Poland – empirical research" is a presentation of the results of own research based on the educational project Contest of Entrepreneurship and Management – OPiZ, in which the participants are the population of secondary school students (previously upper middle school). The project, whose author is Andrzej Brzeziński, has been organised since 2012; currently, it is in its seventh edition, and it also contributes to the economic education of students. Students from leading schools in the national rankings, and also from institutions from small towns, take part in it. The presented research was carried out for the first phase (school) competitions of the VI Contest of Entrepreneurship and Management, in which 3,881 students participated, and 300 people were randomly selected from this population as a sample in which the level of economic knowledge was assessed. The research tool was a questionnaire consisting of 50 closed-ended questions. At the same time, a questionnaire survey was conducted that aimed at the participants' assessment of the achievement of the educational goals of the Contest. A questionnaire consisting of 26 questions was used here, which also served to obtain information about the project participants.

The study ends with a summary, which reviews the implementation of research goals and problems, together with conclusions and guidelines for the continuation of research on the issues raised, as well as the issues of economic education, especially education for entrepreneurship. In summary, we present the verification of our research hypothesis.

1 The need to disseminate economic knowledge of young people in the modern world

1.1 Economic thinking

Aristotle already claimed that man is a social being, and he must live among other people and cooperate with them. Our consciousness and way of life do not develop "by themselves", but are shaped in relationships with other people. This makes us:

- watch them
- imitate and talk to them
- learn to feel, think and react

Thus, a man is a member of various groups and communities (Aronson, 2009: 5–7).

As a member of the community, the family, the clan, he becomes a social being. Social psychology deals with all the relationships that arise on the individual-group line. We are to answer the question of how economic awareness and economic thinking were born. But to answer this question, we must first:

a   explain the concept of awareness and social awareness
b   explain the process of shaping human needs

The word "awareness" has so many meanings that it needs to be considered only from a specific point of view. In our case, we want to come from this word to economic thinking. If so, consciousness is "a mental process with two characteristics and a perspective engaging the contents currently presented in the mind, and the feeling that accompanies these mental contents" (charaktery.eu). This approach to consciousness is very interesting from the point of view of explaining the genesis of economic thinking. Namely, this "feeling that

DOI: 10.4324/9781003206446-1

accompanies these mental contents" is nothing but the relationship of an individual with the outside world. It is a clear clash of the individual consciousness of a particular person with social consciousness (kognitywistyka.net). So what is social awareness? According to Emile Durkheim, social consciousness is clearly different from individual consciousness and is not a simple sum or average of the consciousness of individual members of society, but functions to some extent as an independent phenomenon. Durkheim states that social awareness is a sociological concept and means a set of ideas, symbols, concepts, opinions, views and prejudices common to the vast majority of a given community (mfiles.pl). Thus, it can be concluded that social awareness is a segment of culture as a model of views and ideas that are widely and generally accepted in a given community, which become norms and patterns of thought instilled and enforced. As L.J. Krzyżanowski rightly writes, thanks to signs, symbols and a common convention, and especially, *the language*, people form ideas, views and beliefs. These, in turn, studied, analysed and compared, create simple and complex models and theories. It is the domain of science. When we transfer these theories and models to economic and social life, what we call the application of theory to practice occurs. Only at this point does the phenomenon of social consciousness begin to take shape (Krzyżanowski, 1999: 284). Paweł Sztompka claims that social awareness may have various manifestations and may take various forms:

1   Common-sense thinking – intuitive, somehow internal conviction, often hasty or one-sided. We cannot always verify this thinking. The English use the term common sense here, and the Poles use the term "in layman's terms" (Polish: na chłopski rozum).
2   *Sacred zone*, i.e. ideas and images about the supernatural world, ultimate matters, life after death. It also features magic, myths and religions.
3   Ideologies, i.e. systems of ideas that serve to support, justify and legitimise certain group interests or reinforce group *identity*.
4   Public opinion, i.e. all views on matters common to a given community, e.g. economic, political and social (media, press, radio, Internet).
5   *Knowledge* scientific, i.e. views and beliefs that can be verified, considered true or false by scientific verification or falsification.
6   Artistic creativity (art, literature, music), i.e. products that exemplify human artistic and emotional experiences created for the audience and not for oneself (Sztompka, 2002 295).

When analysing the category of social consciousness, one cannot ignore the phenomenon of pathologies of social consciousness, which occur especially in large communities. We distinguish here:

- stereotypes – that is, simplified and one-sided and generally exaggerated areas of a given phenomenon, person or community, treating the subject in the same, undifferentiated manner
- superstitions – negative, marked stereotypes, formulated towards foreign communities
- group chauvinism – opposing views about the community accompanying stereotypes and prejudices, in which the person formulating the judgement participates, excessively positive (Krzyżanowski, 1999: 291–292)

Social awareness can also be mythologised. How should this be understood? A "myth" comes from the Greek word *mythos*, which means a legend or a story. Most often, it means a certain story, a real or unreal event, but imagined and rooted in the historical memory of a group, community, nation. So, the story told contains both an element of historical truth and fantastic elements. Thanks to this, mythology, i.e. collections of myths, allow historians to learn about the world view, beliefs, rituals and customs of peoples such as the ancient Greeks, Romans, Aztecs, Incas and Mayans. The myths served primarily religious purposes and also tried to explain some:

- natural phenomena
- random events
- history cases (Klp.pl)

Myths refer to experiences, emotions, ideas and superstitions rather than to rational knowledge.

We can also talk about the pathology of social awareness in smaller groups, where group thinking can be seen. As a result of the frequent isolation of such a small group, it is closed "in itself", often called the "surrounded fortress" syndrome. This group then loses the sense of objective reality, and their behaviour becomes irrational. There is a distortion of the external environment, inadequate assessment of oneself and one's own abilities, causing:

- disregard for potential and real threats
- a sense of strength and impunity
- belief in own superiority

- devaluing foreign groups and their leaders
- emphasis on loyalty within the group
- the development of full unanimity as a result of the lack of different opinions than the current one (Sztompka, 2002: 305)

Such group thinking is the most common cause of failure for this group.

Consciousness – from the point of view of medicine and natural sciences – is part of the human psyche that is under his control, it is the ability of a person to know reality and himself, it is the state of mind of a person who is able to receive all information coming from the outside world and it is possessing knowledge about something. The human brain shapes consciousness and uses it for human life. The Great Dictionary of the Polish Language quotes the following statements:

"'consciousness' receives impulses – information from the environment – and must properly process them so that they become understandable".

"There is no world independent of *awareness* of a human. There is no objectively existing matter or energy" (wsjp.pl)

We have analysed the processes of awareness and social awareness. The social awareness of a human being – a social being is always directed both inwards and outwards towards the environment. It can be determined by the *movement of consciousness*. The neurobiologist Antonio Damasio describes this consciousness movement as a process of *thinking* (Damasio, 2013: 103–129). Thinking is a continuous cognitive process of association and inference, operating with memory elements such as symbols, concepts, phrases, images and sounds. Human thinking is realised by cognitive mental processes, based on a system of concepts of varying degrees of specificity, combined in the brain in a more or less conscious way. Thinking is therefore also a brain process that carries symbolic operations, such as:

- associations
- inference
- supporting by subconscious memory search operations (Damasio, 2013: 103–129)

There are many models of general thinking, the most important of which are the models of:

- rational thinking
- irrational emotional thinking
- context-dependent thinking (encyklopedia.pwn.pl)

Thinking can be considered as a conscious mental process of a human being in the broad sense, leading to indirect and generalised cognition and understanding of the surrounding reality. On the other hand, in a narrower sense, thinking is an active mental activity, thanks to which the general characteristics of various things, events and phenomena as well as the relations between them are reflected (encyklopedia.pwn.pl).

Thinking is, according to biologists, neuroscientists, psychologists and psychiatrists, the process of generating new information that serves either *cognition or making decisions*.

This is how we came to the phenomenon of economic thinking. What was the genesis of economic thinking? The primitive man behaved in the primitive community in such a way that he had to satisfy his biological needs. The behaviour of the Neanderthal man (24,500 years ago) was related to the instinct of self-preservation and the satisfaction of biological needs. Hence, it can be concluded that despite the fact that the Neanderthal did not have sophisticated needs, he noticed that nature did not provide him with "free of charge" adequate amount of goods for life. It can be said that there has already been a shortage of goods serving to satisfy the needs, and in a not fully aware manner, the Neanderthal started the decision-making process. For example, he noticed that the fruit that grows high on a tree can be obtained from a branch that fell off the tree. This branch was the first tool for the acquisition of consumer goods. This is how economic thinking began as an unnamed or poorly recognised by researchers' category. Man – with varying degrees of success – began to subjugate nature, following, like the animal world, his instinct for self-preservation. In our opinion, economic thinking was born on two foundations, i.e. the necessity to meet biological needs and the development of social awareness, which led to the emergence between people which created the needs of a higher order.

The genesis of economic thinking is presented in Figure 1.1.

Scheme 1 shows in an extremely simple way the unconscious rise of economic thinking, which began to be consciously described in the Epic of Gilgameus (4,000 years ago), in the Old Testament (over 2,000 years ago) in the Indian Vedas (1,500 years ago and later in such works as "Iliad", "Odyssey", the writings of Plato and Aristotle and later in the works of St. Thomas Aquinas). Today, every textbook on economics or macroeconomics describes in a precise manner, often with the use of a mathematical apparatus, economic thinking as the basic economic category (Sedláček, 2012: 31–39).

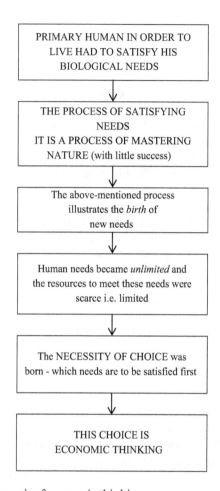

Figure 1.1 The genesis of economic thinking.
Source: Drawn up by Authors on the basis of B. Noga, M. Noga, A. Dejnaka. Edukacja ekonomiczna polskiego społeczeństwa, Issue. II, CEDEWU, Warsaw 2019, p. 12.

Economic thinking can be clearly divided into two stages – the first stage is *unconscious* economic thinking and the second stage is *conscious* economic thinking.

Scheme 2 presents the development of economic thinking in a block-like manner (Figure 1.2).

We will now try to describe the individual steps in the development of economic thinking.

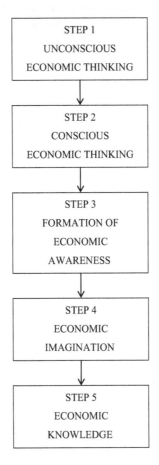

Figure 1.2 Development of economic thinking.
Source: Drawn up by the Authors on the basis of B. Noga, M. Noga, A. Dejnaka, *Edukacja...* op.cit. p. 15.

Step 1 Unconscious economic thinking appeared at a time when the man of the primitive community noticed that nature did not always provide him with goods that would satisfy his biological needs. He then began to accumulate stocks of goods serving to satisfy his biological needs. Such behaviour was practised by the Neanderthal man, and in our opinion, it was the beginning of economic thinking, not fully conscious, because it was caused by the instinct of self-preservation.

Step 2 The transition from unconscious economic thinking to conscious thinking took place at the moment when man, mastering nature, noticed that his needs were constantly growing and eo ipso are unlimited, and natural resources – unprocessed and processed by man – are limited, rare, defined in economics as scarcity. Here, we would like to clear up a few issues:

A   Defining the concept of "economic thinking". There are hundreds of definitions of *economic thinking*. Our working definition of this concept is as follows: Economic thinking is the necessity of choosing scarce goods to meet the unlimited needs of man in such a way that the result of this choice would be the most favourable from the point of view of the preferences of the man making the choice. It is a conscious mental process of a person who must decide in what order and with what intensity they will satisfy their needs, having at their disposal, in specific conditions, an appropriate resource of goods and services.

B   Economic thinking is the economic history of the world, showing how humans mastered nature and developed production processes and the distribution of produced goods and services.

C   The history of economic thinking has shaped:
   • economic awareness
   • economic imagination
   • economic knowledge

which we will cover later, discussing the next steps in economic thinking.

Step 3 The formation of economic awareness is closely related to the development of social awareness as part of culture. The essence and scope of economic awareness can be deduced from the concept of social awareness because economic awareness is related to making decisions regarding the management of resources at the disposal of all entities operating in the economy.

The literature on the subject discusses low and high economic awareness. And such low economic awareness causes:
• irrationality
• inefficiency
• risky decisions regarding the management of own resources (Adamska, 2008: 226–235)

In this monograph, when analysing the problems of economic education of young people in Poland, we should note that it largely depends on the environment in which this education is provided, and this especially applies to households. We can distinguish here households with low economic awareness.

Household with low economic awareness:

- react poorly to the variability of the closer and more distant surroundings
- have little tendency to save
- communicate poorly with the external environment
- are prone to consumer bankruptcy

are not prone to macroeconomic thinking, and their attitudes and ideas about the economy are based on short-term experience, usually a one-off event and microeconomic culture.

In turn, households with high economic awareness:

- are susceptible to stimuli sent by the central bank
- are an active entity in the financial market
- have the ability to think critically, which allows them to make conscious choices, not only economical, but also political (Noga, 2014: 118–120)

Step 4 The concept of economic imagination was introduced by A.K. Koźmiński, stating that it

> is something more than common economic knowledge formed from scraps of economy and political (sometimes electoral) ideology, reaching people through various channels as well as economic and political messages and comments in the mass media. Direct observations and experiences with the real economy of individuals and human groups, elements of morality, religion and political sympathy and attitudes as well as everyday human emotions are decisive for shaping this fragment of social awareness: feelings of insecurity, hope, anger, envy, bitterness, discouragement and fear.
>
> (Koźmiński, 2014)

Step 5 It is the crowning achievement of the development of economic thinking in the form of accumulated and written economic knowledge, shaping such categories in social life as:

- minimisation of expenses
- maximising the effects
- unlimited human needs, especially acquired (cultural) needs in comparison with stable human physiological needs
- changes in human needs in terms of their size and structure
- recognition of production and technical progress as a creator of new needs limited resources:

- for an individual → free time, financial resources, qualifications and professional predispositions
- for the economy → limited resources, factors of production, i.e. labour, land and capital
* alternative cost, always accompanying a choice, understood as the capital of lost opportunities and thus lost benefits as a result of taking a specific decision (solution)
* division of goods into free and economic
* rational management (Noga, 2009)

1.2 The emergence of economy and its development

The development of economic thinking led to the emergence of the science of economics. The genesis of the name "economy" was born in Ancient Greece and was proposed by Xenophon, a student of Socrates, who lived in 430–355 bc Xenophon combined two Greek words:

oikos = home

nomos = law, norm
_____
which gave him: oikosnomos = economy

Oikosnomos as the principles of management in the Greek household were described by Xenophon in his work of the same title. A similar procedure was performed by Aristotle (384–322 bc), and in fact, Aristotle is considered to be the "father" of economics. Why? This is because Xenophon dealt with the division of labour, on a microscale, and Aristotle dealt with the exchange of goods and money, and therefore with economic issues of a much larger scale (Landreth, Colander, 1998).

The modern word "economy" is used in all the languages of the world. So, let us now try to present the cognitive aspect of the word economics, i.e. to what events (phenomena) and what subjects are assigned to the word "economy" by the speaker, and whether it is the cognitive process of that phenomenon or object.

And so *ad rem* – economy is:

1   science that analyses and describes the production, distribution and consumption of goods and services
2   saving time in the process of producing goods and services, in operation in general
3   rationality of action, i.e. action based on reason

4   effectiveness of action, that is, a comparison of inputs with effects
     (benefits) and in a situation when the benefits exceed the inputs by
     means of an identical measure, such action is considered effective,
     that is "economically profitable"
5   a team of all industry economics, i.e. trade economics, cultural
     economics, transport economics and industry economics. In Eng-
     lish, it is simply economics (which in Polish translates as econom-
     ics or as a team of economics or all industry economics)
6   mathematical economics, ecological economics, behavioural eco-
     nomics, institutional economics, classical economics, neoclassi-
     cal economics, liberal economics or illiberal economics, Marxist
     economics, Keynesian economics, microeconomics and macroe-
     conomics, mezzoeconomics and global economics

All of the above-mentioned types of economics are still the science
of economics, where the laws, categories and economic models were
"passed" through the appropriate "filters" of the ecology of a set of
institutions, rules, behaviours, etc. Of course, newer types of economics appear here, such as the economy of culture, socio-economics, or
such research trends, as sociological imperialism in economics and
economic imperialism in sociology (Noga, 2017: 27–35).

The science of economics is a relatively young science because it
appeared at universities only after the Spring of Nations in 1848.

As we have already stated above, the name economy comes from
Xenophon, a Greek writer, general and philosopher, a student of
Socrates, who lived in the 5th and 4th centuries BC. Even so, it cannot
be argued that Xenophon created the new science called economics.
Some representatives of the history of economic thought argue that it
took 21 centuries (2,100 years) for the "real" science of economics to
develop.

In fact, Aristotle (4th-century BC) had a chance to create the new
science "economics" as a completely separate, independent science.
Xenophon did not teach at the Platonic Academy or at Aristotelian
Likeon, and it is widely believed that Aristotle, not Xenophon, introduced the term "economy" as the Greek oikosnomos. But Aristotle
combined economics with chrematistics, i.e. the ability to accumulate
wealth, and with politics, then classified as ethics, hence during Aristotle's lifetime, economics adopted a "purely" ethical character and,
above all, an Aristotelian methodology involving speculative thinking and abstraction. This state of "economy" actually lasted until the
end of the 16th century, when the works of John Locke, Francis Bacon and later French encyclopaedists appeared, and first of all, the

first manufactories or enterprises were created, and in England, a new socio-economic system was born, commonly known as capitalism (Noga et al., 2019: 21–22).

The monograph is a search for an answer to the question: how to teach economics to young people so that they can properly make economic decisions based on economic knowledge, based on objectively discovered and functioning economic laws, devoid of unjustified colloquial judgements, myths and stereotypes of populism. Students of the University of Economics in Wrocław, back in the 1960s, liked to say in a light and witty way that "economics is simple common sense, presented in a complex form". The English, also in the economic journalism of the late 19th century, often spoke of *common sense*, that is, common sense in the management process. This English "common sense" is nothing but the Polish "layman's terms".

Economics as a science developed gradually. From Xenophon and Aristotle in Greece through the economic thought of ancient Rome, St. Thomas Aquinas in the Middle Ages and such trends as:

- mercantilism
- physiocracy
- utopian socialism

Economic considerations were conducted on the fringes of other sciences such as:

- philosophy
- theology
- ethics
- and even astronomy Nicolaus Copernicus wrote about the corruption of money, because "worse money displaced better money from circulation"

This period, lasting more than 2,200 years, is called by historians of economic thought a *pre-scientific period of economic development*. The analyses in this period were spectacularly normative (Noga, 2017: 19–35). This can be explained as follows:

a   in economic considerations, scientific methods such as induction, deduction, experiment, categorical thinking, abstraction and idealisation were not used only by mental speculations, not only on the fringes of theology, philosophy, ethics or astronomy, but even in poetry, for example, in Homer, Gilgamesh and in the speeches of Cicero.

b   while normativeness economic considerations of that period meant that the effects of mental speculation were compared to the prevailing morality (ethics). These speculations were applied to the ethical norms of the society of the period of slavery or of fundamentalism and early capitalism.

The second, higher stage of economic science development is the so-called scientific period of economic development.

The reasons for the transition of economics from the pre-scientific period to the scientific period were:

1   The emergence of the views of René Descartes, John Locke, Thomas Hobbes, David Hume and Francis Bacon. Generally, these views indicated how to conduct scientific research and what to do to make human cognition reliable (objectivity). And so:

–   Descartes (1596–1650) says that the study of reality, including economic reality, must be characterised by clarity and distinctness (*clair et distinct*). Science should be characterised by:

  •   rationality (cogito, ergo sum)
  •   mathematics determining the quantitative properties of the phenomenon
  •   inductive thinking and analysis and synthesis

–   Thomas Hobbes, creator of social naturalism, where human nature is determined by selfishness and self-preservation drive. Man is ruled by the same mechanical laws as nature. By means of deduction, one can also learn the mechanism and laws governing society and the state institution. The institution of the state was created not from man's nature, but from his fear and common sense, forcing him to give up part of his nature and to conclude a special social contract creating a social framework for human rights and obligations. Hobbes formulated the famous principle "homo homini lupus est"

–   John Locke (1632–1704) is promoting:

  •   empiricism
  •   sensualism (experiences gained through the contact of the senses with the environment)
  •   utilitarianism and ethics

In scientific cognition – according to Locke – man is born as a blank page (*tabula rasa*) and only experience, external impressions and

reflection from the observation of oneself referring to the ancient pun-
dai i gnoti seauton lead to the shaping of human nature. Locke is an
advocate of economic freedom, a liberal constitutional state. Locke
pioneered the view that *work* creates value.

- David Hume (1711–1776) recognised impressions as the only
  source of knowledge. Man is a social being from birth. Hume
  places deduction much higher than induction. He is a pioneer of
  the quantitative theory of money and the theory of foreign trade
  (balance of payments).
- Francis Bacon (1561–1626), founder of empiricism and the modern
  scientific method based on the *experiment and induction*. He is the
  creator of the theory of idols or illusions of the human mind:
  • idol tribus (tribal illusion), resulting from human nature
  • idol specus (cave illusion), superstitions
  • idol fori (market illusion), inaccuracy
  • idol theatri (theatre illusion), erroneous philosophical
    speculations

Science must eliminate such illusions. Summing up, our deliberations
on new scientific trends that allow for an in-depth study of economic
reality lead us to the conclusion that science begins to develop *cate-*
gorical thinking. Such thinking is a fundamental prerequisite for the
separation of the science of economics from the world of science. Categorical thinking through induction, deduction and reduction in the
thought process created categories, models, trends and, above all, economic laws (Stankiewicz, 2007: 54–171).

The second prerequisite for the transition of economics from the
pre-scientific period to the scientific period was the emergence of the
Reformation as a new movement, not only religious, but also social.
The Reformation introduced *work ethos* instead of previously propa-
gated *prayer ethos.* Countries that relied on the Counter-Reformation
and remained faithful to the principle of a work ethos as the "key" to
salvation began to develop very quickly, and this process continues to
this day. The Reformation allowed for the emergence of a new socio-
economic system, i.e. capitalism, and in it – a capitalist enterprise.
Then, economics entered the world of science as a separate science
taught at universities. As is commonly known, *the first university was*
established in Bologna in 1158. Subsequently, universities were established in Italy, France, Germany, Austria, the Czech Republic and
Poland. Historically, this development of universities has been as
follows:

University of Paris	1194	Rome	1303
Oxford	1214	Avignon	1303
Padua	1222	Perugia	1308
Naples	1224	Orleans	1309
Toulouse	1229	Prague	1348
Siena	1240	Cracow	1364
Montpelier	1289	Vienna	1365

Originally, universities had four faculties for four majors, namely:

• liberal arts, painting, music, literature (atrium)
• the canonic law
• theology
• medicine

Later the following ones joined:

• mathematics with astronomy
• philosophy
• physics
• mechanics
• the so-called practical fields, that is, ethics, economics and politics

Economics first appeared at a university in Germany, and although both Universität Halle and Universität Frankfurt/Oder were founded in 1727, the Halle Chamber Music Chair was recognised as the first university chair in economics.

In Germany, in the 17th and 18th centuries, cameralistics was an economic doctrine that recognised the guiding principle of state policy (goal), the full use of human resources and production capacity to increase the ruler's income. Cameralistics was a form of mercantilism. Anyway, the full name of the Department at the University of Halle is the Department of Cameralistics, Economics and State Administration. The founder of this department was a professor of history and law, educated at the University of Marburg – Justus Christoph Dithmar (1678–1737), born in Kołobrzeg and educated as a lawyer at the universities of Leipzig and Halle. In Poland, the first department of economics was established at the newly created Faculty of Law and Administration of the University of Warsaw in 1816. In 1818, the department was taken over by Fryderyk Skarbek.

This was the beginning of academic economics. Today, economics is taught at universities, institutes of technology, economics and non-economics colleges – practically at all universities (Bochenek, 2002).

What is the subject of economic research? Usually, the answer to this question is contained in the definition of the science of economics. However, today, we can distinguish at least 20 different trends, schools of economics and each of them has its own definition of the subject of research.

The Economics textbook by Paul Samuelson and William Nordhaus, which has several editions and has been translated into 40 languages, gives several definitions of economics:

- "Economics is the study of human activities related to production and exchange between people".
- "Economics analyses changes in the economy as a whole - trends in prices, production and unemployment. Once these phenomena are understood, it helps shape the policies by which governments can influence the overall economy".
- "Economics is the study of how human beings organise activities in the sphere of production and consumption" (Samuelson, Nordhaus, 1998: 25).

Due to the complexity and multidimensionality of economic science – as the above three definitions show – the definition of the subject of research is constantly evolving. Like other evolutionary sciences, economics collects data, formulates hypotheses and then verifies or falsifies them, which allows it to describe the functioning of the economy.

There is no doubt that despite such a wide range of definitions of economics, economists, influenced by Lionel Robbins' famous 1932 essay, adopted a standard approach to the subject of economics, which reads as follows: "Economics is the science of analysing human behaviour between given goals and limited means with alternative uses" (Robbins, 1932).

This approach to the subject of economic research has gained enormous popularity among economic theorists and is cited all over the world. Each of the schools of economics, giving its definition of its subject, refers to the definition of L. Robbins. The popularity of L. Robbins in terms of the subject of economics results from the fact that economics tries to solve it in this definition *the problem of choice*: what rare means – with an alternative purpose – to use to achieve goals that may change over time? (Noga, 2009: 9).

However, it should be noted that the definition of the subject of economic research by L. Robbins is based on the so-called neoclassical methodological individualism, which:

- refers to the research of Adam Smith, the creator of classical economics, who assumed that economic units are mainly guided in their behaviour by their own, self-defined interest (egoism).

The problem is described by the concept *homo oeconomicus*, which states that man minimises the distress and maximises the pleasure in all his actions

• assumes that all phenomena and processes and the corresponding economic categories should be "in the last resort" deduced from the economic behaviour of individuals

The development of society and economy in the 20th and 21st centuries meant that man cannot rationally define an ordered set of his preferences because, today, there is no perfect, cost-free access to all information shaping such a set of human preferences. In management, "uncertainty is the most certain", therefore, in order to objectively describe the economic reality, the economy must – apart from methodological individualism – use methodological holism, which in management will take into account the logic of choosing social groups, societies deciding on the use of scarce resources that may have other alternative applications, in order to create various goods and divide them into the present and future concept between different people and different groups in society (Noga, 2009: 9–10).

Contemporary economics, which includes in its research programme the problems listed above, is divided into microeconomics and macroeconomics. Microeconomics deals with the study of economic phenomena and processes occurring in individual areas of the economy, for example, in a specific market. Microeconomics studies the behaviour of business entities such as a household and a business. The central problem of microeconomics is the way in which individual decisions are coordinated by the market mechanism in the markets of consumer and production goods in the labour market and in the financial markets. Microeconomic analysis aims to explain the mechanism of using scarce resources in the market economy.

The production and consumption processes analysed by the microeconomic theory take place in the conditions of competition, the determinant of which is the presence of the closer and further external environment. The processes of economic choice must therefore be preceded by an analysis of the social conditions of the production of goods and services and therefore another economic entity – the state – appears on the economic scene. The behaviour of the state as a subject of management is the subject of macroeconomic studies (Noga, 2009: 12).

Macroeconomics examines the national economy as a whole or its main components, presenting a broad panorama of economic activity. Macroeconomics does not deal with details such as the relation of the price of bread to the price of milk or the relations of supply and demand in a given market, but it deals with the problems of increasing the production of goods and services throughout the country, employment and unemployment, the inflation rate, etc.

The difference between microeconomics and macroeconomics is more than just the difference between small-scale economics and large-scale economics. The aim of the analysis of both sciences is different. Microeconomics mainly studies – at the appropriate level of abstraction – specific markets, while macroeconomics deals mainly with the connections between different parts of the economy. So, in macroeconomics, building blocks are used to build different models to explain how they fit together and how they influence each other. Therefore, in macroeconomics, we use, for example, broad aggregates such as aggregate demand, aggregate supply, money demand, money supply and inflation (Noga, 2009: 13).

The monograph is intended to contribute to the economic education of Polish youth *sui generis*, that is, a specific, special type of educating young Poles in the field of economic knowledge and its application in the economic practice of households, enterprises, sectors and industries of the economy and the operation of the state as an economic entity. Therefore, we present below what we think the structure of a microeconomics lecture should be:

1   the emergence of economy and its division
2   research area of microeconomics
3   the management process and the decision-making process
4   the functioning of the market mechanism
5   household as a consumer of goods and services. The laws of supply and demand. Elasticity of demand and supply
6   the company as a provider of goods and services on the competition:
    a   perfect
    b   monopolistic market
    c   on the oligopolistic market
7   cost and income analysis in the short and long term
8   markets of the factors of production – labour, land, capital (Noga et al., 2019: 25–26)

In turn, typical and, in our opinion, extremely useful for understanding the contemporary problems of the national and global economy – the lecture on macroeconomics should have the following structure:

1   introduction on Macroeconomics and economics, research area of macroeconomics

2 the role of the state in the economy
3 system of national accounts. Macroeconomic measures
4 models of economic growth
5 investments and their distribution
6 state fiscal policy. Unemployment
7 monetary policy of the state. Inflation
8 macroeconomics of an open economy
9 AD–AS general equilibrium model
10 IS–LM general equilibrium model
11 cyclical development of the economy. Globalisation (Noga et al., 2019: 26)

But last not least economists studying the economic reality around us *discover* certain *tendencies, trends, regularities, cause and effect relationships*, learn the nature of these observations and on this basis and formulate *economic laws*. Economic laws are scientific laws, but in relation to the laws of nature, i.e. the laws of physics, chemistry, biology and mathematics, they show their very *specific features.*

The economist studies the cause-effect relationships occurring in the management process.

A typical cause-effect relationship is described by the relationship:

A (cause) → B (effect)

Someone will say that this is an obvious relationship! But while in physics, chemistry, biology and mathematics, one specific cause A always and everywhere produces the effect B, and in the economic process, a specific cause A may cause the effect B, C, D, etc. In the natural sciences, we are dealing with deterministic laws which mean that one cause produces one specific effect, while in economics there is one cause and many effects. This is the economic uncertainty. Based on our research, we try to determine the probability of the effect B occurring as a result of the occurrence of cause A. When we determine this probability, we find that we have discovered the economic law.

Note to readers undertaking to learn the ins and outs of economics. Economics is the science of human behaviour, and people are different and therefore behave differently. Moreover, the same people in the same situations, *but at a different time*, do not always behave the same way. While studying human behaviour and their cause-effect relationships, economics must investigate, measure and describe all these events. When 70% of cause A produces effect B, most economists say that we have discovered an economic law. Why? The answer is given here by statisticians who say that when we study mass phenomena, then in the case of researching a scientifically selected sample, achieving about 70% of the effect B, as an effect of the occurrence of cause A, allows us to formulate a specific *stochastic* law of just this sample. The remaining 30%, .e. the effects of C, D, E, F, G, etc. are a random factor (component) defined as two standard deviations that represent approximately 30%.

O. Lange, P.A. Samuelson, D. Begg, N.G. Mankiw. M. Blaug and many others claim that economic rights are as follows:

1   They can be discovered and formulated only during the study of a large number of phenomena, and hence we call them the laws of large numbers. In individual cases, the economic law cannot be discovered.
2   They are objective in nature because although they concern human behaviour, they are independent of people's consciousness and will.
3   They are *statistical* or *stochastic* laws, i.e. the studied, significant relations, regularly occurring in economic processes, do not always show a relation where the cause A causes the effect B because there are "deviations" from this relationship, which make up the random factor tested by means of variation and standard deviation, as already discussed above.
4   They are historical in nature, which means that, at some point, they work, then they stop working and new economic laws appear in their place (Blaug, 2000; Samuelson, Nordhaus, 2010)

In the literature on the subject, the following types of economic laws are distinguished:

- cause and effect
- functional or otherwise, represented by a mathematical apparatus, most often by means of a function
- coexisting laws, i.e. that certain economic laws coexist with other economic laws
- people's laws of behaviour (react to stimuli)
- the law of the intertwining of human activities (exchange of the results of their activities)
- Technical-balance, i.e. the relations of inputs and outputs terminated by a specific technique (Lange, 1959)

Here, we come to a comparison between the laws of nature and the laws of economy. Natural laws are deterministic, which means that one specific cause always and everywhere produces the same effect. Of course, the researcher of the laws of nature takes into account everything, under what conditions the cause-effect relationship occurs, i.e. pressure, temperature, type and structure of materials. The laws of nature are hierarchical in nature, which means that secondary laws are based on fundamental rights (Noga et al., 2019: 32). The fundamental differences between economic laws and natural laws are therefore as follows:

1   Natural laws are deterministic and very precise, which can be represented by a mathematical apparatus, and economic laws are stochastic laws, which simply means that one cause (precisely defined) can produce different effects, although one of these effects will occur very *often*, e.g. 70% of times or more.
2   Natural law can be discovered by examining a specific *single* case, while the economic law can only be discovered with *mass* occurrence of the phenomenon under study.
3   Economic laws are historical in nature, that is, they start to work, they work and cease to work, and natural laws work *eternally* and anywhere on the globe.
4   There is no doubt that economists would like to deal with deterministic economic laws. However, the analysis of the nature of economic phenomena and the area of research in the science of economics that we have carried out clearly indicates that economics, when studying human behaviour, states that:
    a   The same people behave differently at different times and in different places.
    b   In the same place and time – *hic et nunc* – different people in the same situations behave differently.
    c   The combination of a and b also takes place continuously.
    d   In addition, the economic laws of the intertwining of people's actions and people's behaviour operate as a reaction to **stimuli, stimulants** (Noga et al., 2019: 32–33).

Economics discovered *specified* economic law, acting like all economic laws, that is, in a stochastic manner and formulated them as a cause-and-effect relationship.

Cause P → produces effect S

The practical use of such an economic law consists in the following:

1   If the result **S** has a positive effect on the growth of social welfare (individuals and society), we should strive to have as many **P** causes as possible because there is a high probability of a positive **S** effect in the economy.

2   If the **S** result has a negative impact on the welfare of society and the economy, everything must be done so that there is no **P** cause. Eliminating the **P** causes with a high degree of probability will eliminate the negative **S** effect.

It is *primary* economic knowledge for the whole society. There are no understatements or "loops" here, but there is something else. Man likes "black and white" situations, the occurrence of certain events, and that is not what the economy is able to provide. Until market participants, i.e. everyone becomes convinced that "the most certain thing in the economy is uncertainty", and that there is a risk in making every economic decision, and they will not make rational decisions (Noga et al., 2019: 33).

1.3 The ability to use economic knowledge by young people in the family, on the market, in society

In order to use knowledge at all, one needs to know the basic canons of a given science that we need to use to satisfy our needs. In the era of digitisation of the economy, we do not have to perfectly remember all categories, laws, formulas, cause-and-effect relationships, but it is enough to be able to use the Internet and especially the literature on the subject presented on the Internet.

For this, you need:

- consumer education
- financial education
- entrepreneurship education
- macroeconomic education

We will describe how to educate young people in Poland in the field of economics in the following chapter of this monograph. We will compare the education of young people in Poland and in the world there. However, even before the presentation of the content of the process of economic education of young people in Poland and in the world, we would like to present some principles of shaping the ability to use economic knowledge. The discussed problems are the result of the didactic experience of the authors of this monograph and research on the usefulness of the application of economic theory in economic practice.

Below, we present the "clash" of several economic theories with practice.

1.3.1 Investors' behaviour on the stock exchange

The stock exchange reached its mature shape in the 19th century, although its origins are traced back to the 16th century. The stock exchange is a regulated market on which transactions of purchase and sale of various financial instruments admitted to trading are carried out, and above all, the marketability of securities, e.g. shares or bonds, and derivatives, e.g. futures and options (m.xelion.pl). The stock exchange is a place where companies and individual investors buy shares through specialised brokerage offices, which is regulated by stock exchange regulations. Experts studying nearly 100 years of share price developments on the stock exchange stated that:

a   If you want to invest based on the change in the price of a stock and make a profit on these trades, buy stocks when their prices go down and sell these stocks when their prices go up. Experienced players – stock market investors do this. And how does Jan Kowalski, who watches the stock exchange and hears from his neighbours that they earned, for example, PLN 100,000 on the shares of the company "X" because the share prices of this company began to rise rapidly, Kowalski does not listen to economists that now "X" shares need to be sold, not bought and he BUYS "X" shares. After a very short time, the prices of "X" shares begin to fall rapidly, and Kowalski again does not listen to economists and sells "X" shares, instead of, just then, buying them. The effect is that Kowalski has suffered losses, and he in turn tells his neighbours that investing on the stock exchange is not worth the hustle. In order to invest on the stock market, one has to listen to economists, not to neighbours, and this is a very good example of how to use economic knowledge (and how not to).

b   In the theory of economics, there is the phenomenon called *perspective theory*. Let's explain this with an example:

   Event A. A customer comes to a clothing store with the intention of buying a winter sweater for around PLN 150. There were several dozen sweaters at this price and in various colours, sizes and types. But, in the same store, there was a seasonal discount for sweaters, where the old prices were written on their labels, crossed with a line and the new prices were given. Among these discounted sweaters, there was a sweater with the old price of PLN 400 and the new price of PLN 200, which meant a PLN 200 discount. What did the client do – he bought this sweater for PLN 200 despite the fact that there were several dozen sweaters for PLN 150 of the same quality and in different colours. What was the client's reasoning here: although he spent PLN 200, he allegedly "earned" PLN 200 because he bought a sweater, which previously cost PLN 400, for that amount. He could also reason like this: I pay PLN 50 more for this discounted sweater, but it cost PLN 200 more than I paid for it, I allegedly earned PLN 150. And event B explains what the reality is.

Event B. The situation is similar to event A, only the customer passed this store because he did not notice it, he then entered the next clothing store and there were no seasonal discounts on winter sweaters, he easily bought a sweater for PLN 150, of very good quality and in his favourite colour.

What is the conclusion: in event A, the client succumbed to the so-called prospect theory and compared to the event B lost PLN 50 or incurred PLN 50 higher costs of purchasing a sweater.

Conclusion of the authors of this monograph: when you buy certain goods, remember about the theory of perspective, you will save money that you can spend on increasing your standard of living (Noga, 2017: 48–51).

c In addition to the mainstream of economics, often called ortho-dox, there is also a non-orthodox current of economics, in which there are many schools including:
- behavioural economics
- experimental economics
- socio-economic theory
- neuroeconomics
- evolutionary economics

It is behavioural economics that studies deviations from rational management resulting from the mainstream *homo oeconomicus* model adopted by economics. The *homo oeconomicusa* model assumes:

- full, free information about the action taken by a human
- management is extracted here from:
  - history
  - interpersonal relations and the functioning of society (Noga, 2013)

Under these conditions, man makes decisions that are not "maximis-ing" but satisfactory decisions of "bounded rationality", as described by Nobel laureate Herbert Simon (Landreth, Colander, 2002).

On the other hand, behavioural economics lists a number of anomalies, which are deviations in human activity from rational management:

- a man in his conduct applies *framing*. This means that, for example, he considers losses and benefits separately
- sunk costs effect – people are inclined to stick to the decision made, if it was associated with a significant expense
- ownership effect – assigning more value to things that can be created than to things that can be gained
- status quo effect – reluctance to lose the state of affairs or change it
- disposition effect – avoiding grief caused by loss and striving for pride caused by profit (Tyszka, 2010: 35)

The examples of the economic theory-economic practice relationship presented above show that there is a rich resource of economic research on a functioning economy. Decision-makers in any economic entity (household, company, institution, NGO, foundation, company, etc.) may try to take advantage of the achievements of the economy. But it is known in advance that economics is not a natural science, and one cause A can produce not only the desired effect B but also the effect C, D, E, F, G, H, etc. Therefore, based on that, myths and stereotypes arise. The most common stereotypes and myths are:

SM1 – business (entrepreneurship) cannot be learned.
SM2 – economic knowledge is so complicated that only a few can not only get to know it but also be able to use this knowledge.
SM3 – private entities, getting to know the economic risk and having knowledge about risk measurement, will only try to reduce the risk. Risk reduction alone does not guarantee business success.
SM4 – only small businesses are flexible, agile and alert. These features are also shared by medium and large enterprises.
SM5 – in households, economic decisions are made by one person. Of course, this is the case only when the household is run by a single person, while in multi-person households we are dealing with group decisions that have their own specificity (Noga, Noga, 2019: 140–141).

2 Formal and informal methods of economic education of young people in Poland and in the world

2.1 Acquiring economic knowledge by young people in the European Union and in the world

Education and vocational training policy in the EU is one of the areas that fall mainly within the scope of the Member States' potential. However, the EU has adopted a number of European and global programs to support such vocational training.

In the Treaty of Maastricht of 1992 defining the functioning of the European Union, Article 150 states:

Community action shall be aimed at:

- facilitating adaptation to industrial changes, in particular through vocational training and retraining
- improving initial and continuing vocational training to facilitate professional integration and reintegration into the labour market
- facilitating access to vocational training and fostering the mobility of trainers and learners, especially young people
- stimulating cooperation in the field of education between educational or vocational training institutions and enterprises
- developing exchanges of information and experience on issues common to the education systems of the Member States (eur-lex. europa.eu)

In 2018, the European Parliament adopted a resolution on the modernisation of education in the European Union, where points 103–112 define the tasks of the Member States in the field of vocational education, with particular emphasis on entrepreneurship. This resolution says:

103 We encourage the Member States and the Commission to create a system of innovative and flexible subsidies aimed at fostering

DOI: 10.4324/9781003206446-2

artistic and sports talent and abilities in the field of education and vocational training; support the Member States that intend to introduce scholarship systems for talented students in education, sports and arts.

104 In this regard, we welcome the Commission communication on a new skills agenda for Europe (COM (2016) 0381), which proposes a solution to the skills mismatch and gaps and measures to develop an appropriate skills recognition system; in this context, we encourage Member States to develop high-quality dual education systems (of great importance for overall personal development and for the development of skills for lifelong learning) and vocational training in cooperation with local and regional entities and according to the specific nature of each educational system; we note the advantages and growing attractiveness of a hybrid educational system combining both robust school and vocational education tracks.

105 We recommend strengthening educational counselling as an important instrument for making a flexible transition through different education systems, while at the same time enriching and updating the person's knowledge and skills.

106 We support and encourage educational and career guidance as a key task of education for the personal and social development of young generations.

107 We believe that entrepreneurship is an engine for growth and job creation as well as a way to increase the competitiveness and innovation of economies, which helps to empower women.

108 We stress out that social entrepreneurship is a growing field that can revitalise the economy while reducing poverty, social exclusion and other social problems; we therefore believe that entrepreneurship education should include a social dimension, addressing topics such as fair trade, social enterprises, corporate social responsibility and alternative business models such as cooperatives in order to pursue a more social, solidarity and sustainable economy.

109 We call on the Member States to focus on entrepreneurship and financial education, volunteering and language proficiency and to prioritise these skills in vocational education and training programs.

110 We call on the Commission and the Member States to promote specific employment opportunities linked to vocational training and education and their relevance to the labour market.

111 We call on the Member States to develop career guidance to facilitate the identification of pupils' and students' skills and aptitudes and to support a tailored learning process.

112 We draw attention to the specific educational situation of children and young people whose parents travel in Europe for work purposes and call on the Commission to carry out a study aimed at examining the specific situation of these children and adolescents in terms of the challenges they face in pre-school and school education (sip.lux.pl).

At this point, we would like to point out that, in the USA, Japan and also in the so-called old EU countries (Germany, France, Italy, Belgium, the Netherlands), when talking about economic education, one thinks primarily of teaching entrepreneurship, in particular, it concerns teaching entrepreneurship to children and young people (Greene, 2020). As rightly considered by K. Wach, the USA and the so-called Western countries pay special attention to "entrepreneurial education for entrepreneurship", as shown in Figure 2.1.

In order to achieve the intended effectiveness of education for entrepreneurship, there must be a kind of synergism of educational programs (formal education) with informal forms of extracurricular or extra-academic education. School and university education for entrepreneurship must therefore be supported by the institutional environment, in particular, by the broadly understood economic practice. The effectiveness of education for entrepreneurship is implemented through successive stages (QAA, 2012: 9–12):

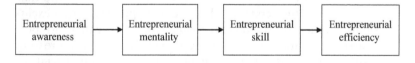

Entrepreneurial education for entrepreneurship should include three integrated components, namely (Heinonen, Poikkijoki, 2006: 83):

- learn to understand entrepreneurship (knowledge)
- learn to be entrepreneurial (skills)
- learn how to become an entrepreneur (attitude)

The aim of education for entrepreneurship, which includes the transfer of knowledge, acquiring skills and shaping attitudes, is to foster entrepreneurship (entrepreneurial attitudes) in the personal, social and professional lives of learners (Figure 2.2). In practice, it allows

EDUCATION FOR ENTREPRENEURSHIP

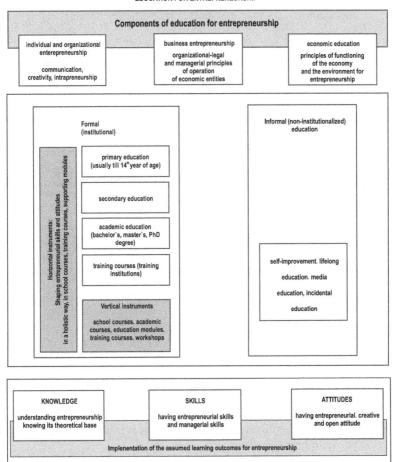

Figure 2.1 Structuring education for entrepreneurship.
Source: Drawn up by the Authors on the basis of K. Wach, *Edukacja na rzecz przedsiębiorczości wobec współczesnych wyzwań cywilizacyjno-gospodarczych*, Wyd. Uniwersytetu Ekonomicznego w Krakowie, Kraków 2013, Przedsiębiorczość – Edukacja No. 9

learners to discover, learn and experience the mechanisms of process entrepreneurship that determine the achievement of the desired goals of entrepreneurship education. As a result of such a programmed education process, learners shape their entrepreneurial personality, which is manifested in proactivity and innovation, readiness for changes and action, that is, active initiative (Frederick et al., 2020).

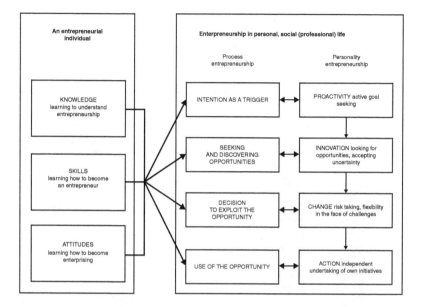

Figure 2.2 Entrepreneurial education process for entrepreneurship.
Source: Drawn up by the Authors on the basis of K. Wach, Edukacja...op.cit.

Education in the USA, a country with a definitely free market economy, is as follows:

a   It is possible to study in private and public primary and secondary schools and universities.
b   Primary school is usually for children from six years old and lasts eight years. From four to six, the children go to a kindergarten.
c   Secondary school lasts usually six years divided into:

– The so-called junior high school (or middle school).
– Senior high school (a student during the first three years of high school is a "junior" and in the last three years he is a "senior").
– Regardless of the system, primary and secondary education ends at the 12th grade at the age of 17 or 18. After graduating from high school, the student receives a high school diploma, the equivalent of our Matura exam, and can apply for admission to a university (poland.us).

- In the USA, from kindergarten to high school diploma, a student is educated in a creative way of entrepreneurship, and this is the basic domain of economic education in the USA.
- Professor Erkko Autio, co-author of the study, notes that:

The United States are at the forefront of entrepreneurship development because authorities know that entrepreneurship plays a key role in the US economy. When we combine it with the culture of determination and motivation, we have a recipe for success.

(Acs et al., 2016)

Americans also focus on innovation. They are capable of producing products and services that no one else can. The development of entrepreneurship is not hindered by even the high cost of broadband in the USA compared to other countries (biznesnaostro.pl).

The European economy is far from the American one in terms of its approach to entrepreneurship. This poor position is due to the European mentality. And since Polish entrepreneurs are brought up in the culture of our continent, we reproduce many negative attitudes that make it difficult for us to catch up with the Americans.

The Educational Development Centre in Warsaw, in cooperation with the European education information network EURYDICE (eurydice.org.pl), has prepared the "Review of educational systems in 9 European countries" as part of the Project co-financed by the European Union under the European Social Fund, which concerned the following countries:

1 England
2 Wales
3 Scotland
4 Ireland
5 Germany
6 The Netherlands
7 Spain
8 Romania
9 Czech Republic

This project has the same structure for each of the surveyed countries and includes:

•   the structure of education, compulsory schooling
•   basics of teaching

- about supervision
- about the teachers
- interesting things (ore.edu.pl)

While reading this document, you will notice that:

- Curricula show great autonomy of primary and secondary schools.
- Of course, *entrepreneurship* is an obligatory element of the curriculum here because practically, in all surveyed countries, attention is paid to adapting students to life in society through the transfer of knowledge and skills and equipping an individual with tools for acquiring knowledge.
- In the studied countries, there is a strong bond between secondary schools and higher education institutions (universities), which allows young people to shape their professional orientation. Secondary schools in these countries are often involved in research organised by universities.
- In another study by the Educational Development Centre in Warsaw, Jerzy Wiśniewski, as part of the European project "Improving the strategy of education management at the regional and local level, wrote that:" The educational policy of the European Union... does not exist, but it works, How? In this report, the author included two scenarios of the future of education (Table 2.1).

Table 2.1 Scenario of the future of education

Status quo	School from scratch (*re-schooling*)	Without school (*de-schooling*)
Strengthening the bureaucratic school system	Schools as social centres	Learner networks in a network society
Extension of the market model	Schools as learning organisations	Escape of the teachers – "*meltdown*"
Maintain a (strong) bureaucratic school system	Schools as social centres	Learner networks in a network society
	Schools as learning organisations	Escape of the teachers – "*meltdown*" Extension of the market model

Source: www.ore.edu.pl/polityka-ue-jwi.pdf, accessed on May 29, 2020.

How to understand the categories used in these scenarios:

2.1.1 *Learners network*

Widespread disappointment with school and the emergence of new opportunities led to the rejection of the school system.

Networks created by parents, organisations and religious associations.

Some local, others collaborating internationally.

Small groups, home schooling, individual solutions.

Limited role of management instruments and settlement of results *(accountability)* and use of strong, inexpensive ICT.

The profession of a "teacher" disappears. The boundaries between a learner and a tutor and teacher and parent are blurring. There are new specialists for the student.

2.1.2 *Social centres*

Schools are recognised as an effective safeguard against the breakdown of social ties. Clearly defined tasks for the local community. Shared responsibility with other institutions and organisations. Using sources of knowledge and experience.

Various organisational forms. Emphasis on informal learning.

High level of funding – ensuring good conditions for education everywhere *(learning environments)* and the high prestige of teachers and schools. Intensive use of ICT, especially for communication and cooperation in networks *(networking)*

Core – professional teaching staff, various forms of employment, good wages. Many associates around the "core".

2.1.3 *Market model*

i   Widespread dissatisfaction of "strategic clients" led governments to withdraw from direct involvement in schools, widespread use of market mechanisms, promoting differences.

ii Many new education providers, fundamental changes in funding rules, incentive system. Schools survived.

iii Choice is paramount – when it comes to "purchasing" educational services and when employers judge their value. Emphasis on cognitive skills but also values.

iv Growing importance of "market currencies": indicators, accreditation are replacing public monitoring and curriculum regulations.

v   Widespread innovation, "painful" transformations and inequalities.
vi   New learning professionals – public, private, temporary....

Source: www.ore-edu.pl/polityka-ue-jwi.pdf, accessed on May 29, 2020.

In its various documents, the European Union states that the following educational professions should be completed as early as 2020 in education policy:

- implementation of the concept of lifelong learning and mobility
- improving the quality and efficiency of education and training
- promoting equality, social cohesion and active citizenship
- increasing creativity and innovation, including entrepreneurship, at all levels of education and training (eur-lex.europa.eu)

Now, we show how youth entrepreneurship is created in Ottawa. This case is a role model in other cities and countries, which is why we read it in its entirety.

Youth entrepreneurship benefits the economy by creating jobs, increasing competitiveness, creating innovative goods and services, creating a strong community and cultural identity and generating revenue. This is due to our research and from research presented in the literature of the subject. However, creating youth entrepreneurship requires support from the state and other public authorities, e.g. regional city authorities and local authorities. A good example in this regard is the Canadian city of Ottawa, which has prepared 76 programs for young people under the age of 30 undertaking business activities. Among these programmes are, for example, programmes for:

- kindergarten to high school
- high school and undergraduate
- undergraduate
- graduate and undergraduate
- graduate
- postgraduate and graduate
- postgraduate (Daze et al., 2009)

For our research conducted in this book, the first two programs listed in this list are of particular interest.

"Youth Entrepreneurship: Ottawa's Portfolio in Talent Development" was developed by a team of researchers from S. Daze, M.

Sharma, L. Lalande and S. Riahi in 2007. Sonia Riahi, assessing this program, concluded that it brings the following benefits to Ottawa:

- creating employment
- providing local goods and services to the community, thereby re-vitalizing it
- raising the degree of competition in the market, ultimately creat-ing better goods and services for the consumer
- promoting innovation and resilience through experience-based learning
- promoting a strong social and cultural identity
- continuously creating and growing diverse employment opportuni-ties different than the traditional fields available in a particular city

The client survey from the Ottawa Centre for Research and Innova-tion (OCRI) Entrepreneurship Centre indicates that 43% of their cli-ents in 2008 had started a business or were still in business during that year, with almost half of the participants having been in business for over two years. The clients reported more than $166 million in new investment into their business and an estimated $247 million in total sales. The report also shows a net result of 2,996 jobs created, with an average of 3.5 new hires per business (excluding the founder). Of the clients surveyed, 29% were aged 30 years or younger, indicating that youth entrepreneurs are actively using entrepreneurship support avail-able to them and are actively contributing to the local economy, at the very minimum, through income generation and employment cre-ation (Riahi, 2010). In her assessment, S. Riahi compares youth entre-preneurship and draws the following conclusions: Though youth and enterprise share many of the same characteristics, such as resourceful-ness, initiative, drive, imagination and ambition, youths have an in-creased number of challenges when compared to adult entrepreneurs in terms of launching and running a new venture:

- less access to capital, whether it be personal savings, investments from family and friends or access to loans from financial institutes
- less experience and a narrower range of experiences
- lack of access to workspace
- less extensive network of contacts
- reliance on simple tools or no equipment at all (Riahi, 2010)

Comparing Ottawa's youth entrepreneurship programs as a whole to the best practices of successful youth entrepreneurship programs presented in the subject literature, Ottawa scores well on the following criteria:

- well-trained and properly supported staff
- flexible operation styles
- reliance on local business specialists
- initiative-based
- mentoring
- equity and diversity
- government involvement
- integrated packages
- proper targeting and selection of clients
- introducing commercial orientation to universities (such as the technology transfer offices) (Riahi, 2010)

Our assessment of the youth entrepreneurship support programme shows that there are multilateral benefits here. On the one hand, the city provides its residents with very good satisfaction of needs, and on the other hand, young people gain not only the first income but also gain business experience.

These principles bring special attention to the role of entrepreneurship and its education at all levels of education and in all European countries, not only EU members, which of course also applies to Poland.

2.2 Formal economic education of young people in Poland

The Central Economic Information Centre informs that, in Poland, there are:

- a total of 2,645 public high schools
- a total of 1,684 private high schools
- a total of 1,764 public technical high schools
- a total of 325 private technical high schools
- a total of 3,006 post-secondary schools (coig.com.pl)

According to the estimates of the authors of this monograph:

- over 30% of technical high schools are economic, commercial-economic, economic-tourist, IT-economic high schools, etc., which gives the number of about 650 public and private economic technical high schools

- over 50% of post-secondary schools, i.e. more than 1,500 such schools, are post-secondary economic schools

The Introduction to Business course appears in secondary schools in all its types: high schools, vocational schools and technical high schools. In the most popular type of secondary school in Poland, attended by the vast majority of students, i.e. high schools, the Introduction to Business is implemented in the amount of two hours in the first grade. This means 60 hours of teaching this subject. For comparison, history is taught for 380 hours, mathematics 1070 and Polish language 1320. In classes with managerial or similar profiles, there may be an additional subject called economics, in practice developing the issues raised on the Introduction to Business. The Introduction to Business also appears in post-secondary schools, where you can obtain the title of a technician. Some elements of knowledge about economics and entrepreneurship are also learned by students in middle schools during Civics – but this will obviously change with the liquidation of middle schools. Moreover, elements of entrepreneurship are included in the course of Civics. The Introduction to Business course is usually taught by non-economists. Only 42% of teachers in this course have an economic education. The remaining teachers have different professional background. They can be teachers of the Polish language, physical education or biology, quickly converted into teachers of the Introduction to Business. It is enough to complete postgraduate studies completed in three or sometimes even only two semesters and you can already teach another course. The motivation of teachers is even worse. Only 20% of teachers teach the Introduction to Business because of their interest in this field of knowledge. It must be admitted, however, that as many as 89% of them believe that the knowledge provided during this course is needed (money.pl).

This is the picture of formal economic education in Poland. On the other hand, in high schools with an economic and business profile, the curriculum is shaped as follows:

A   All general education courses provided for high schools by the Minister of Education, except that three subjects, i.e.
- maths
- physics
- geography

have an extended curriculum

B   The general courses will be accompanied by courses corresponding to the fields of study and the profile of the profession adopted

in a given high school. A typical high school with an economic and business profile includes:
* financing and management
* economics/microeconomics + macroeconomics
* selected industry economics
* marketing
* accounting (small bookkeeping)
* logistics
* management and IT management support
* decision-making theory
* real estate market

By undertaking activities in the field of economic education, we expect that understanding the mechanisms of the market economy will help us to function successfully in the conditions of this economy. At the same time, we bear in mind that theories formulated in the field of social sciences are not absolute. In particular, in the field of economics, no assumptions about economic behaviour are absolutely true, and no theoretical conclusions are valid always and everywhere. In the economic world, however, one can observe a certain order that results from transactions made by entities seeking to maximise their own benefits. Formulated on this basis, they are useful tools for solving problems in this area of human activity.

In this situation, the basic task is to identify those factors that are of key importance for building modern human life strategies. Professional work still remains the central category with its economic dimension. Nowadays, the main issue in human life is to prepare for a profession that allows you to take a specific place in social life. The essence of this process has its fully economic dimension. On the one hand, we are dealing here with a specific educational investment, and on the other, with an offer in the form of knowledge, specific skills and competences, having a specific price on the labour market. The educational and social policy of states focuses on this form of human activity. This is due to the belief that education is one of the most serious instruments decisive for the implementation of strategic goals of modern societies (Szewczuk, 2000: 235; Sikora, 2011: 17–33).

Research on the state of knowledge and economic awareness of children and youth in Poland shows an insufficient level of economic knowledge among this group of Poles. Therefore, governmental and non-governmental organisations, media and social media undertake activities aimed at increasing the scope of economic knowledge of young Poles, which will be analysed in the following subsection.

2.3 Informal methods of acquiring economic knowledge

In June and July 2018, the National Bank of Poland (NBP) conducted a survey of the state of knowledge and economic awareness of children and adolescents in Poland on the following sample:

- sixth-grade primary school students 600 people
- students of the third grade of junior high school 600 people
- students of the penultimate years of senior high school 600 people
- parents of students 600 people

The results of these studies are as follows:

I   Subjective assessment of the level of economic knowledge
  - At each educational stage, students critically evaluate their economic knowledge. Regardless of the stage of education, only about 5% of students assess their knowledge as large or very large.
  - The results of the objective test show, however, that it is not so low.
II Objective assessment of the level of economic knowledge
  A   Sixth-grade primary school students versus financial and economic knowledge

Average of correct answers in the test:

- 57%

The most commonly used sources of knowledge:

- talking to the family
- courses at schools
- TV programs

Most preferred sources of knowledge:

- class discussions
- playing a financial game in the classroom
- watching movies

Most preferred topics:

- saving money
- Internet banking
- career planning

The student with the greatest deficiencies:

- lives in the countryside or in a city with 50,000 up to 200,000 residents
- lives in the southern region (Małopolskie, Opolskie, Śląskie and Świętokrzyskie voivodeships)

The greatest gaps in economic knowledge:

- definition of GDP
- definition of inflation
- retirement age in Poland

The greatest gaps in economic skills:

- understanding the terms of deposits
- calculation of interest on a deposit

B   Third-grade junior high schools students versus financial and economic knowledge

Average of correct answers in the test:

- 58%

The most commonly used sources of knowledge:

- courses at schools
- online websites
- talking to the family

Most preferred sources of knowledge:

- class discussions
- setting up your own mini business
- playing a financial game in the classroom

Most preferred topics:

- investing money
- career planning
- starting your own business

The student with the greatest deficiencies:

- lives in the eastern region (Lubelskie, Podkarpackie, Podlaskie voivodeships)
- lives in the central region (Łódzkie, Mazowieckie, Wielkopolskie voivodeships)

The greatest gaps in economic knowledge:

- currencies and exports
- bond profitability and the state of the economy
- guiding rates and interest on loans

The greatest gaps in economic skills:

- understanding the terms of deposits
- calculation of interest on a deposit

C   Students of the penultimate years of senior high school versus financial and economic knowledge

Average of correct answers in the test:

- 58%

The most commonly used sources of knowledge:

- courses at schools
- talking to the family
- online websites

Most preferred sources of knowledge:

- class discussions
- group discussions
- setting up your own mini business

Most preferred topics:

- starting your own business
- career planning
- investing money

The student with the greatest deficiencies:

- lives in the central region (Łódzkie, Mazowieckie, Wielkopolskie voivodeships)
- lives in the northern region (Kujawsko-pomorskie, Pomorskie, Warmińsko-mazurskie voivodeships)

The greatest gaps in economic knowledge:

- bond profitability and the state of the economy
- currencies and exports
- guiding rates and interest on loans

The greatest gaps in economic skills:

- understanding the terms of deposits
- calculation of interest on a deposit (NBP, 2019)

Among the 28 recommendations resulting from the survey, the NBP considers the most important:

- Attitudes related to being a **conscious consumer and employee** and an **entrepreneur** should be shaped. It is important to present practical knowledge about banking products, rooted in family experience, but also the dangers of using ill-considered credits or loans. It is necessary to introduce basic economic and financial concepts into the teaching process. The educational offer should include topics that interest students: investing money, saving, planning a professional career and starting your own business.
- Economic knowledge can be made more interesting and easier to understand for students of secondary/senior high schools by linking it to **students' areas of interest** (e.g. sports, music, computer games, fashion and travel), i.e. explaining economic issues based on examples from the areas of interest of students. For example, currently, their interest is in cryptocurrencies or obtaining financing for business activities. Accordingly, their needs and interests should therefore be **systematically diagnosed**.
- It's worth to **link the sources of economic knowledge** used by students so that the family, school and media complement each other. It would be good if parents and teachers could draw the content needed for the economic education of children from the media. The students themselves can also learn about economics from the media – from the Internet or television. It is worth showing them (also through teachers and parents) sources of interesting and reliable educational materials.
- Parents – the main "source" of money for students and schools (by educating about saving methods and assumptions) should **coordinate their actions**.
- At this stage of education, it is worth explaining complexities in **macroeconomic relationships**.
- The main channels for reaching students should be **family and school courses** (Civics and Introduction to Business) as these are the most frequently used sources of economic knowledge. Another good channel of reach is also the **Internet** because this medium is used by the vast majority of students every day (NBP, 2019).

Similar research was conducted by Bartosz Majewski, and he concluded the results of his research as follows:

> The study revealed that the economic maturity of students from the last years of primary school and the first years of junior high school is low. The most poorly understood categories of terms are macroeconomic issues with which respondents come into contact primarily through the media. Knowledge in this area is disordered, full of distortions and simplifications, based on myths rooted in society - unfortunately, with the high frequency of macroeconomic concepts among respondents, the false belief that these concepts are well known to them is reinforced. This thematic scope should therefore be treated with special attention in educational programs, both in formal education and in activities undertaken by non-school institutions.
>
> (Majewski, 2011)

Better understood among the surveyed group are the terms with which the respondents have the opportunity to encounter in their everyday life, e.g. when participating in conversations in their households or in economic events with which the given terms are related. However, a better understanding of the concept does not always translate into the ability to use knowledge in practical behaviours, especially when it requires a synthesis of skills from other disciplines (hence, for example, the inability to mathematically calculate the percentage of investments, or to explain the mechanisms of economic crises historically). For this reason, when thinking about teaching economics, it is worth considering its interdisciplinary connections with other subjects to a greater extent (e-mentor.edu.pl).

In Poland, as part of economic education activities are undertaken by NBP, School Savings Bank (SKO), PKO BP bank, Bank Foundation of Leopold Kronenberg Citi Handlowy Bank as well as the dynamically developing and gaining more and more participants Children's Universities of Economics and the Academies of Young Economists. Many other organisations or foundations (e.g. www.ekonomianaulicy. pl, Foundation for Economic Education), the article is limited, however, to the description of those national initiatives with the longest history (e.g. SKO) and in which education is the main area of their activity (e.g. economic universities).

As part of its educational function, NBP runs an economic education portal, addressed mainly to junior high school and high school students, teachers and students. The portal contains not only current economic information but also a dictionary of economic terms, popular science articles and multimedia presentations. It should be noted that the news posted on the portal is provided in an accessible form, illustrated with many examples, so that it is as understandable as possible for a young recipient and it encourages further contact. The discussed portal also includes simple games, checking, e.g. knowledge economic terms, as well as decision-making, in which the player aims to obtain the greatest profit from the conducted activity. Through playing, the participants gain economic knowledge (e.g. puzzles of various notes and coins or crosswords), and in practice, they get to know the reality of the functioning of economic entities on the market, which aims to stimulate entrepreneurial attitudes and behaviour among young people. An extremely important part of the discussed portal is the e-learning platform, which offers free training in the field of micro or macroeconomics, investment basics or the principles of rational incurring financial liabilities as well as financial analysis of the company. The NBP website is the largest educational platform in Poland, the content of which is used not only by pupils and university students but also teachers of economic courses (the portal contains lesson plans) (nbp.portal.pl).

The oldest financial education programme in Poland is the School Savings Bank under the patronage of PKO BP, established in the 1920s. Like the NBP economic education portal, it is a unique initiative in Europe, and the world aimed at helping children and young people develop the competences of personal finance management, shaping the habit of saving and gathering knowledge on this subject as well as acquiring practical skills in using banking services. SKO is addressed to students under 13, offering the first Internet banking service for children in Poland (Goszczyńska et al., 2012: 125).

Economic education is also a priority area of activity of the Banking Foundation established by the Citi Handlowy Bank of Leopold Kronenberg. The Foundation carries out its projects in cooperation with other entities (e.g. the NBP, the Youth Entrepreneurship Foundation and the network of WSB Universities), and they concern, among others, economic education of children and youth (the programme "From a grosz to a zloty" implemented as part of integrated education in grades 1–3 and "My finances" – an economic education programme run jointly with the NBP and addressed to school students). Part of its activity is also addressed to students of senior high schools who plan to continue their education in the field of economics and, in the future, to choose a profession in the financial industry. The program consists of three parts: Financial Knowledge Contests like "Banks in Action", the Entrepreneurship Day, during which students are invited to the bank's headquarters to learn about the work of a banker and workshops enriching knowledge about the principles of banking institutions. In addition, the foundation also initiates educational programs targeted at adults (e.g. "A week for saving") and, together with the NBP, initiates activities to develop a draft of the National Financial Education Strategy. The activities carried out by Citi Handlowy are an attempt to transfer the experience of the Citi Foundation to Poland, which promotes financial knowledge in almost 100 countries around the world (Goszczyńska, 2012: 120–138).

An extremely valuable initiative in the field of economic education are the Children's Universities of Economics, established and developing in the last few years, addressed to students of the fifth and sixth grades of primary schools and the twin Academy of Young Economists, which is an economic education programme for junior high school students. The organiser of these undertakings was the Foundation for the Promotion and Accreditation of Economic Studies together with several economic universities (SGH Warsaw School of Economics, University of Economics in Katowice, University of Economics in Poznań, University of Białystok). These activities are also under the honorary patronage of the Ministry of Education. As part of the university as well as the academy, one-semester long, free courses are organised for participants. During one semester, there are six two-hour meetings devoted to management, economics, marketing, economic history, psychology and business ethics. At the same time, knowledge is conveyed in a manner adapted to the young recipient and also reinforced with multimedia presentations. These meetings are interactive – participants gain knowledge during discussions, teamwork and games.

The websites of both initiatives also contain a knowledge base consisting of presentations from individual editions of the courses as well as other materials available free of charge (uniwesytet-dzieciecy.pl; gimversity.pl).

Another interesting idea are proposals of training courses for parents in the field of developing entrepreneurial skills in children and adolescents, conducted by economic universities in Poland.

In Table 2.2, we present access channels to economic knowledge in Poland.

Urszula Sierżant and Wiesława Kitajgodzka developed a programme entitled "Economic education at school. Why is it worth

Table 2.2 Access channels and forms of educational activities

No.	Access channels	Forms of conducting educational activities
1.	Media (press, radio, television, Internet)	Educational and information campaigns: – broadcasts on TV and radio (including the so-called *idea placement*), – press supplements, – multimedia materials (presentations, films, economic games), banners, streams, surveys, available on websites
2.	Publications	– serial and non-serial publications, – brochures, – multimedia publications
3.	Public debates	Conferences, seminars, debates
4.	Contests	Competitions concerning economic knowledge, subject contests, competitions for the best academic thesis (master's, doctoral, habilitation)
5.	Studies	Academic studies, postgraduate studies
6.	Training	Training courses, workshops, lectures, courses, training games, distance education – e-learning, coaching and mentoring
7.	Entrepreneurship Academies	Small manager, Finance for young people, Marketing, etc.

Source: Own work.

implementing the Economics in everyday life program?" The authors assumed that:

> Each student should have basic knowledge and skills in managing their own resources. This applies to making decisions and planning activities, setting priorities, predicting results based on the available information and, above all, managing your finances.

Therefore, we propose to include the programme "Economics in everyday life" in the school curriculum. In 2017, the Minister of Finance of the Republic of Poland also submitted a project for all secondary schools entitled "Economics and Finance". We think that the project of U. Sierżant i W Kitajgrodzka is extremely interesting.

The most important reasons influencing the need to include the Economics programme in the school's didactic and educational programs can be expressed in the following points:

1   The modern, rapidly changing world creates great opportunities for human development, the possibility of taking up an interesting

job; but at the same time, it requires constant adaptation to new market needs. Omnipresent competition forces a young person to make a lot of effort, use the full knowledge and skills to be able to achieve the intended goals.

2   For every human being, the basis for functioning in a market economy is the ability to make rational decisions and predict the effects of one's own actions.

3   The dynamically changing reality makes it necessary to flexibly manage personal finances and to regularly adjust the home budget to new family and professional circumstances. It happens that young people educate their parents in this field.

4   Shaping consumer awareness brings benefits for society and the economy and allows avoiding many social risks and costs resulting from rash actions of people.

5   Economic education programs make it possible to learn about the laws of economics and the basic mechanisms of the market economy to become familiar with the basic economic terms and the role and operation of various financial institutions and instruments (junior.org.pl).

Thanks to the implementation of the programme, young people participating in it:

- gain elementary economic knowledge
- learn the principles of business operation and their practical application
- learn about the principles of safe use of electronic banking
- shape the skills of managing own finances
- learn to use the rights of consumers
- get to know themselves (their strengths and limitations) and the rules of creating an image
- gain the ability to plan and predict the effects of their own actions
- understand the transmitted content and not only master it in a memorable way
- develop the ability to see various types of relationships and dependencies (cause-effect, time)
- increase the sense of influence on one's own life
- shape the habit of planning activities and rational time management
- gain knowledge of the basics of interpersonal communication, teamwork skills
- learn to adopt a creative attitude towards tasks and encountered problems

- develop the skills of processing and selecting data and assessing its usefulness to solve specific problems
- can make the right choices that create the greatest probability of success (junior.org.pl)

An excellent instrument for shaping the economic knowledge of Polish youth are school Business Incubators (BIs), a pioneering undertaking in Poland, which is a result of academic BIs, highly rated in global business.

2.4 School business incubators

Economic education of Polish schools' students may be conducted in a non-standard way, for example, by establishing and running school business incubators (BIs). The history of BIs is not long, as its origins date back to the end of the 20th century.

Business incubators are organised economic complexes covering a wide group – separated and based on real estate, with a housing offer and an offer of services supporting small and medium-sized enterprises. The operation of such complexes is aimed at supporting the development of newly established companies and optimisation of conditions for transfer and commercialisation of technology by providing space suitable for the needs of economic activity, services supporting business, e.g.

- economic, financial, legal, patent, organisational and technological consulting
- assistance in obtaining funds
- creating the right climate for starting a business and implementing *innovative* projects, the so-called synergistic effects
- contacts with scientific institutions and evaluation of innovative projects (mfiles.pl)

Teaching economics and economic sciences, as we have already described, can take place in a non-standard way, through active participation in an economic activity, where there is a contact between theory and practice. It goes without saying that the first attempts here have been to involve students in business through spin-offs and spin-outs. The first ones were the creation of companies of students and young university employees who set up a new enterprise outside the university. The second ones were spin-outs, also composed of students and university employees, registered and controlled by the university.

There is no doubt that these forms of student activity made it possible, first, to confront the acquired knowledge with business practice, but on the other hand, students gained business experience. These were the reasons for the establishment of BIs. However, young entrepreneurs creating a new business had to look for answers to the following questions from the very beginning:

1   Is the selected business profile the one that you really want to run (now and in the next few years)?
2   Do you have enough strength and energy to do this?
3   Does your state of health allow it?
4   Are you willing to work longer than eight hours, perhaps give up a part or all of your vacation?
5   Does your family understand what it means to run a business and does it accept it?
6   Do you have family support?
7   Are you willing to give up other, often important things to implement the idea (Flis, Makiewicz, 2010: 13–14)?

A small business owner who is just starting his market activity has to reconcile many different obligations. From efforts to understand the market and find ways and factors to stand out in it; by finding answers to the question of who the customers are (market segments), searching for them, serving them and building relationships; right up to setting goals and determining the path to be followed by the company. These issues may be difficult even for an experienced entrepreneur, and for a person with a lack of experience, they are often an insurmountable obstacle, which results in the termination of the company's operation (Pikuła-Małachowska, 2016: 83–90).

The first BIs were established in 1959. Their creator was Joseph Manusco. From that moment until the mid-1980s, it is considered the first generation. It was focused on dividing office space and resources. The second generation lasted until the mid-1990s and focused on gaining knowledge, helping local entrepreneurs and offering them valuable training and courses. Before the start of the third generation that continues today, there were 1,500 incubators. The decisive factors in the development of the idea were the digitisation and implementation of knowledge-based economies and low-resource economies. In 1990, the first BI in Poland was established (European Meeting Centre – Nowy Staw Foundation, ETÖK, Union Haddiema Maghqudin (UHM) 2016: 5–6).

The activities of incubators are very specialised and relate directly to supporting the creation and development of new enterprises. In the case of incubators, special emphasis is placed on aid aimed at innovative companies. Support offered to companies is provided in the initial stage of their existence and, depending on the statute of the organisation, may last from about one to several years. The Offer of Incubators can vary widely and depend on the resources and scale of activities of the centre. However, a classic incubator should offer infrastructure for conducting business activity on preferential terms as well as consulting and training support in a different scope. From a point of view of beginner entrepreneurs, another important factor is appropriate selection of the incubator residents who can provide mutual assistance services which give them additional benefits. Institutional Variety of academic entrepreneurship support centres and their ever denser network make it possible to increase the intensity of activities for the development of the economy in Poland. A big role in this respect is played by EU funds which become the main source of funding for academic entrepreneurship centres.

The market of BIs in Poland is divided into two main groups: local and national incubators. Local incubators operating in municipalities and technology parks specialise in supporting the local community through training and micro-grant programs. Nationwide incubators such as Business For everyone Foundation remotely support business activities throughout the country by lending their legal personality, which makes it possible to run a business and issue invoices without the need to register a business and pay high social security contributions. Incubators of this type often also offer legal assistance, training and conference rooms. In practice, the first BIs were academic BIs.

Academic Business Incubators (ABI) are a response to the market needs for running your own business.

AIP is the largest network of Incubators in Poland, which is a unique *system for testing business ideas.*

The basis of the vision of the future is the awareness and conviction that we need a new quality of supporting entrepreneurship in Poland by helping to establish and develop small and medium-sized enterprises and creating innovative business ideas that are to constitute a competitive advantage of the Polish economy (http://www.inkubatory. pl, available on 16/05/2014).

Academic BIs – this largest academic initiative of recent years was created in 2004 and is still developing today. Its main goal is to develop entrepreneurship among Poles of all ages. The organisers' activities focus on encouraging young people to be active and entrepreneurial.

The AIP offer can be used by any adult (at any age) who does not run a business on the free market and applies to the Incubator with the desire to start their own business and, as a consequence, will be approved for their business idea.

AIP implements the program of pre-incubation (according to the Dictionary of Innovation:

> pre-incubation or a hatchery is the initial stage of the business incubation process, and the pre-incubators created to support this process are the youngest type of entrepreneurship innovation centres). They are most often created within universities and constitute an extension of the didactic process in the field of entrepreneurship with the possibility of preparation for practical operation on the market and verification of knowledge and skills in one's own company.

These specialised units play an important role in serving the needs of potential entrepreneurs at the seed stage of enterprise creation (pi.gov.).

AIP is a network of 40 incubators offering a package of innovative services *with high market and technology potential*, run by the directors of AIP, coordinating activities in their regions and caring for young companies on a permanent basis.

AIP operate at the best universities in Poland in such cities like Warsaw, Łódź, Gdańsk, Olsztyn, Ełk, Szczecin, Bydgoszcz, Toruń, Włocławek, Poznań, Płock, Lublin, Kielce, Częstochowa, Opole, Kraków, Chorzów, Katowice, Rzeszów and Bielsko-Biała. There are over 1,400 developing companies operating in the Academic Business Incubators (inkubatory.pl).

Academic Business Incubators help in the realisation of entrepreneurial dreams and in running your own business by supporting and providing all kinds of help from A to Z.

AIP is a place where in the:

• easiest
• fastest
• least risky

way any young person can start a business (you can check in practice if and how my business idea works).

A young entrepreneur does not need to have a venue or a thick wallet. A good IDEA is enough! *and consistency in the actions taken*, which most often is missing (s.inkubatory.pl).

We are now moving to analysing the formation and operation of school business incubators. Our research shows that while academic Business Incubators were focused primarily on the implementation of innovation, creativity and new solutions proposed by science into economic practice, school Business Incubators primarily support secondary schools in the process of economic education. Of course, school business incubators are also business start-ups, but their emergence is not necessarily related to running a business and gaining a livelihood. Usually in these school incubators there are students who continue with higher education in other cities and it would be difficult for them to run an incubator and study. It should be noted that initially school business incubators were established at vocational schools, which resulted from the specificity of this type of school. However, other secondary schools at that time created entrepreneurship clubs, which were the beginning of school business incubators in the entire secondary education in Poland. Entrepreneurship clubs have transformed into business incubators in such a way that practitioners of the labour market and local entrepreneurs undertook cyclical activities with young people on starting and financing business activities, business planning, project management and using European funds (file: /// E: / School Business Incubators CWRKDiZ in Konin, accessed on July 12, 2020).

The so-called youth policy is the responsibility of individual states and of the entire European Union. It is part of the European Youth Strategy to provide young people with the best possible learning conditions and to facilitate entry into the labour market. The European Commission, wishing to provide those responsible for shaping youth policy with reliable and up-to-date information, has created the Youth Wiki – an online encyclopaedia whose aim is to present the current state of youth policy in Europe. The Youth Wiki encyclopaedia covers eight areas of the EU-adopted document *European cooperation in the youth field (2010–2018)*:

- **education and training**
- employment and entrepreneurship
- health and good condition
- involvement
- volunteering
- social inclusion

- youth and the world
- creativity and culture (Youth Policy in Poland. Encyclopedia KE Youth Wiki vol. 1, 2019).

Business incubators at vocational schools and other secondary schools in Poland are created taking into account the following principles:

- Establishing BIs at vocational and other secondary schools is complex. It depends on the circumstances and whether we are dealing with a public or private institution. It is also important whether the incubator is to be established from the funds of a local government unit from external funds or on the initiative of another entity. There is also the question of the addressees of the project. It is necessary to answer the question whether the incubator is to be established for students of vocational schools or also for their graduates.
- Let us use Art. 21a point 3–4 of the Act of September 7, 1991 on the education system (i.e. Journal of Laws of 2004.256.2572). As a rule, schools and institutions take the necessary steps to create optimal conditions for the implementation of teaching, educational and care activities as well as other statutory activities to provide each student with the conditions necessary for his development, improving the quality of work of the school or institution and its organisational development. These activities can be performed, inter alia, by creating conditions for the development and activity of students and cooperation with parents and the local community. Stimulating students' activity may take various forms, and there is no doubt that it may also involve activation in the form of establishing a BI at the school.
- A public school is a budgetary unit of a commune. Therefore, it has the resources of the commune to the extent that they will be transferred to it for the purposes for which the school was established. Therefore, the commune would have to be the source of financing for a project consisting in establishing a BI. In the case of a private entity, the situation is quite different. A private school runs commercial activities. Financed from subsidies, but also from private owners' funds, it would be up to them to make the final choice as to the legitimacy of creating this form of activity.
- The Act leaves no doubt that the above considerations concern the activation of students. Therefore, it would not be justified to incur this type of investment in order to create start-ups for graduates. But is it in every case? This is certainly the case with the financing

of a new incubator by the commune. However, it is possible to obtain financing from external funds, mainly from European funds. The participation of graduates of vocational schools and other secondary schools in these incubators should not make legal and formal obstacles, as EU funds are available to everyone.

- The functioning of a Business Incubator, even to stimulate students' activity, requires appropriate premises. If the entity is established on the initiative of the school, it should be able to provide it with accommodation. In the case of co-financing activities from external funds, the project budget should provide for rental costs. It is the same in a situation where the premises would be leased by another investor. As a rule, the principal is the person responsible for managing the school property. This is due to the Act on the Education System referred to above. However, it should be remembered that renting the premises belonging to the school's resources for a period longer than three years requires the consent of the competent commune council expressed in the form of a resolution. Some educational institutions have internal regulations that prohibit concluding lease agreements for a period longer than provided for in the regulations, for example, one year. Therefore, before starting an incubator, a potential initiator should think over the plan and ensure adequate logistic security of the investment.
- It seems that, in the case of incubators located at vocational schools and other secondary schools, we cannot speak of any specificity. An incubator can take the form of a foundation as well as a commercial company. It uses the school's infrastructure on a commercial basis and uses its human potential, revealing students' talents on the level of economic activity. School incubators, on the other hand, will be more limited in this respect. For if they operate as part of the school's operation, implementing its statutory objectives as an educational institution, they will not constitute a separate entity. The school is a budget unit of the commune (see Lipiec et al., 2016: 13–46).

School BIs, just like other BIs, need the following support:

1 Support in the field of formal and legal aspects of establishing and running a business
2 Supervision of the company's finances
3 Providing floor space and technical infrastructure for business
4 Support in the field of marketing services

Financing of school BIs may come from:

1 Grants from Labour Offices
2 PARP (Polish Agency for Enterprise Development) grants
3 Seed Capital Funds – Venture Capital
4 Crowdfunding, that is, from funds obtained on social media platforms
5 Business Angels Funds
6 Regional operational programs controlled by Marshal Offices (szkolnafirma.pl)

In September 2019, the Centre for Craft Support, Dual Education and Vocational Training in cooperation with the State Higher Vocational School in Konin, the Regional Development Agency in Konin and the County Employment Office in Konin launched the project "School Incubators of Entrepreneurship" (SIP) intended only for students and graduates of the following secondary schools:

• Mining and Energy Schools Complex in Konin
• Construction Schools Complex in Konin
• Centre for Continuing Education Schools Complex in Konin
• Complex of General and Vocational Schools in Zagórów
• Vocational Schools Complex in Słupca
• Technical Schools Complex in Koło
• Technical Schools Complex in Konin
• Construction and Vocational Schools Complex in Konin.

This project has been implemented with very positive results in terms of the mission of school business incubators. Similar incubators were established in Zabrze, Bytom, Leszno, Poznań, Kalisz, Nowy Sącz, Małopolska and Silesia and where there are academic business incubators (Multan, Walczuk, 2020).

2.5 Myths and stereotypes in shaping entrepreneurial attitudes among Polish youth

In Table 2.3, we have included selected OECD recommendations regarding education policy, and in Table 2.4, the basic principles to consider in designing effective economic education programs.
Information contained in Tables 2.2 and 2.3 should warn against various myths and stereotypes.

Table 2.3 Selected OECD recommendations concerning education policy

Government and other stakeholders should promote objective, ethical and coordinated financial education.

- Financial education should start in schools so that people are educated about it as soon as possible.
- Financial education should be a good practice in financial institutions, which would increase their credibility.
- Financial education should be clearly separated from commercial communication;
- Appropriate rules of conduct for employees of financial institutions should be developed.
- Financial institutions should ensure that the client reads and understands the information, especially when it relates to long-term obligations or financial services with potentially significant financial consequences; small print or incomprehensible documentation should not be used.
- Financial education should focus on particularly important aspects of personal finance, such as basic forms of savings, indebtedness, insurance and pensions.
- Programs should be geared towards building financial capacity (*financial capacity*) and, where appropriate, targeted at specific segments and tailored to individual needs.
- Future pensioners should be made aware of the need to assess the applicable public and private pension arrangements.
- National information campaigns, specific websites, free information services and services warning of high-risk issues (e.g. fraud) for consumers using financial services should be promoted.

Source: "Recommendation on Principles and Good Practices for Financial Education and Awareness. Recommendation of the Council". OECD, July 2005.

Stereotype 1: Risk aversion and failure disrespect culture

The American ethos of an entrepreneur for whom failure is normal in running a business. The more failures an entrepreneur has, the more often he is considered to be more ambitious and courageous.

In Germany, however, similar cases are met with misunderstanding, often with contempt. Looking at the business culture of Italy, it is easy to see that bankruptcy gives a man, and for the rest of his life, a label of someone who will not be able to build something big. Even buying a house or a new car may be a big challenge for him. All this leads to the fact that successful entrepreneurs often have the reputation of unscrupulous capitalists who earn money by exploiting others.

Table 2.4 Basic principles that should be considered when designing
effective economic education programs – communication from the
European Commission

Principle 1. Economic education should be actively supported and should
be made available on a continuous basis at all stages of life.
Principle 2. Consumers should acquire economic and financial knowledge
as early as possible. Competent national authorities should consider
including this knowledge in training programs as a compulsory course.
Principle 3. Economic education programs should include general tools
to educate participants about the need to expand their financial
knowledge and enhance their risk assessment skills.
Principle 4. Financial knowledge provided by entities offering financial
services should be made available in a fair, transparent and impartial
manner. It is important to ensure that consumers' interests are always
respected.
Principle 5. Those directly following the economic education program
should receive sufficient resources and appropriate training to enable
them to carry out the training effectively and with confidence in their
own abilities.
Principle 6. Coordination at a national level among stakeholders should be
promoted to achieve a clear division of labour, facilitate the exchange
of experiences and use available resources rationally and appropriately
according to priorities. International cooperation between entities
offering financial education programs should also be improved to
facilitate the exchange of best practices.
Principle 7. Economic education program providers should periodically
evaluate and, if necessary, update their programs to ensure that they
always conform to best practices.

Source: "European Commission Communication on Economic Education", Brussels,
18 December 2007.

Observing Polish and foreign entrepreneurs, it is very difficult to
find those for whom business failure is an expression of enormous ambition and courage. The environment cannot separate their financial
failure from the personal qualities of such people. We still too rarely
learn from the failures of others; we underestimate those entrepreneurs who, wanting to build a professional business, did not successfully complete this project.

Stereotype 2: No second chance culture

Recovering from a business failure is extremely difficult and painful in
Europe. Entrepreneurs must show exceptional resilience and fight the
pressure imposed by the environment. In the USA, it is believed that
any business that is opened after previous failure has a greater chance
of success.

Stereotype 3: Lack of self-confidence

Compared to the Americans, we still have too little faith in our own abilities. We can laugh at the attitude of "grinning with their beautiful white smiles" New Yorkers or residents of Texas, but note that, from an early age, they have been learning the attitude of "Yes, I can".

Stereotype 4: Self-employment is a risk, we are too conservative

Although the number of self-employed people (micro-entrepreneurs) already exceeds 3 million, as one of the previous texts wrote, most of these enterprises are simply companies established to provide services to one or two clients. Few people are brave enough to take the risk and build bigger businesses. The fear of failure is so strong that Polish entrepreneurs are afraid that if they fail, they may even have a problem with going back to full-time employment. Because they will be considered failures. And if so, it's better not to start at all.

Stereotype 5: Lack of economic education and unstable law

Young Poles often think that:

a   entrepreneurship cannot be learned;
b   the law must change because the environment of economic processes is turbulent.

These are myths. Entrepreneurship can be learned, and the law does not have to change that often. It is enough to ensure a uniform and transparent interpretation of the law. When it needs to be changed, it will not be done as often as in a situation where each Tax Office interprets the same legal regulation differently. No business can accept this in any country.

A good instrument for shaping the economic knowledge of Polish youth is the Contest of Entrepreneurship and Management, which we will present in detail in Chapter 3.

3 Economic knowledge of students in Poland – an empirical study

3.1 Contest of entrepreneurship and management as an educational and research project

The Contest of Entrepreneurship and Management is an educational and research project whose author is Andrzej Brzeziński. It is a project included in the economic contests, thanks to meeting the requirements of the Regulation of the Minister of Education and Sport of January 29, 2002 on the organisation and conduct of competitions, tournaments and contests (Journal of Laws of 2002, No. 13, item 125, as amended). Their participants are students of secondary schools (previously senior high schools) from all over Poland. In the case of exceptionally talented students, at the school's request, the President of the Contest may also allow younger students, i.e. from primary schools (previously junior high schools), to participate, and this was the case in the II OPiZ.

The main goal of the Contest is to increase interest in economic issues and to provide additional economic knowledge to understand the economic processes. It is also supposed to awaken and strengthen entrepreneurial attitudes and behaviour among young people. The program and rules of the competition in the Contest are defined in the *Regulations of the OPiZ* (www.olimpiada.wz.pcz.pl), and the President of the Contest is responsible for the substantive preparation and course of the competition, supported by the Main Committee, the Organising Committee and the Program Council. Each edition has its own theme, which is related to specific objectives as well as the prevalence of questions in the "theme" area. The main topics of each edition and the number of participants in the project are presented in Table 3.1.

I OPiZ was organised in the 2012/2013 school year, and the project became regular with a new edition every year. Currently, the eighth edition of the Contest is taking place. Students from eight voivodeships of

DOI: 10.4324/9781003206446-3

Table 3.1 Main topics and the number of participants in each edition of the Contest

Edition	Topic of the edition	Quantity participants [thousand]
I OPiZ	*Small business*	1.6
II OPiZ	*Family business*	2.1
III OPiZ	*People in the organisation*	2.7
IV OPiZ	*Finance in the enterprise*	4.9
V OPiZ	*Turbulent business environment*	4.7
VI OPiZ	*Entrepreneur in the modern economy*	5.2
VII OPiZ	*Problems of modern enterprise management*	4.2

Source: Own work/

southern Poland took part in the first edition. In the following years, the number of voivodeships increased, and since the fourth edition, it has been a nationwide educational project in which schools from all Polish voivodeships have participated. With each edition, the territorial range and the number of participants increased, and in the VI OPiZ, it exceeded the level of 5,000 students. Due to the fact that the project is not financed by the Ministry of Education, like similar projects, but only supported by the acquired sponsors, no actions are taken to further increase the number of participants. Since the IV OPiZ, the Contest has also become a research project in which the project is evaluated in terms of achieving educational goals, and the economic knowledge of students is examined.

The Contest is an individual competition, and participation in it is free of charge and voluntary. It is a contest consisting of three steps (stages):

- first stage – school
- second stage – regional
- central stage – finals

Of course, with each competition level, the difficulty of the competition questions increases, and the number of points obtained decides about the advancement of students to the next stage. The competition schedule takes into account the calendar and the specificity of the school year. The results of the competition and all information is posted on the website of the Contest: www.olimpiada.wz.pcz.pl and also on the Facebook fanpage: (www.facebook.com/ IVOPIZ/?fref=ts, accessed: June 21, 2020).

The first stage of the contest is held in schools entered into the competition, and students registered by guardians – teachers of the subject

"Introduction to Business", who are responsible for the proper course of competitions at school, maintaining contacts with the organiser and taking care of a group of students participating in the further rounds of the contest. The competition takes the form of a written test with 50 closed-ended questions (see Brzeziński, 2018) and lasts 60 minutes. The thematic scope of the questions significantly exceeds the school curriculum within the subject of "Introduction to Business" and requires extended economic knowledge supported by knowledge of current events in economic life.

The second stage of the contest is held in several districts, and in the case of VII OPiZ, there were as many as nine. Universities and Partner Schools are invited to organise these competitions in individual districts, and these are the University of Economics in Wrocław and the Kozminski University in Warsaw as well as schools whose students achieved great results in the Contest. This group includes XIV High School in Wrocław, High School No. III in Lublin or High School No. III in Gdańsk. Depending on the number of participants and the level of the contest, between 500 and 700 students take part in this competition. Here, just like in school competitions, we've got a test consisting of 50 closed-ended questions. Fifty students with the best results pass to the third stage of the competition, which takes place at the organiser's premises (WZ PCz). The final competition consists of 50 closed-ended multiple choice questions and ten open-ended questions to be done in the same time as the previous competition, i.e. 60 minutes. The winner of the Contest is the participant who obtains the highest score in the third stage of the competition.[1] Apart from the general competition, there are also other categories. Those are "*I have the widest knowledge*", Where the winner is the participant who obtained the highest score in all stages of the competition (total points). The participant from the youngest group, i.e. the first graders, is also awarded (category "*The best among the first graders*").

The Contest also makes it possible for schools to compete in two categories for the titles of:

1 "*Enterprising school*" – the school with the largest number of participants in the first stage
2 "*The best school*" – a school whose students receive the highest total score in the third stage

The "Entrepreneurial school" category is usually where schools that are not highly ranked, also compete and get a chance to earn their place in the history of the competition normally dominated by the leading schools in the country. All schools from the top ten of the "*Prospects* ranking"[2] participated in the last editions. It is mainly these schools that win the second category of the competition.

The events accompanying the Contest are important in achieving educational goals. It is primarily a series of meetings with business people under the common title "Successful people of business", held from the first edition. Among the guests, there were famous entrepreneurs, family business owners such as Andrzej Blikle or Zbigniew Grycan and Zbigniew Jakubas – one of the richest people in Poland. There was also a successful sportsman, Adam Małysz – the most popular Polish athlete.

Additionally, during the first and second editions, a course and a speed-typing competition were organised. On one hand, it is a contribution to computer science education, which in the case of correct or touch typing is ignored in schools. On the other hand, the texts used both in learning to type and in the competition were economic, which is another contribution to economic education.

Another activity accompanying the Contest are educational classes called "Entrepreneurship workshops", conducted by the President of the Contest. These classes are conducted from I OPiZ and take place in schools that have been successful both in the competitions between students and schools. The addressees are therefore students of the school:

- which has won the "Best School" category
- whose student is the winner of the Contest
- whose student is the winner of the "Częstochowski Olimpijczyk" category[3]

Since the VI OPiZ, the winners with the best results have the opportunity to participate in professional internships at the companies of the Impel Group in Wrocław. It is a contribution to the development of the best students.

3.2 Research methodology

The research of students' knowledge was carried out among participants of the first stage of the VI OPiZ. Totally, 5,272 people registered for this edition, and the final number of participants was 3,881. The list included students from leading schools in Poland, such as Secondary School No. 14 in Warsaw, Secondary School No. 13 in Szczecin or Secondary School No. 14 in Wrocław. There were also schools functioning at universities (High School at the SGH Warsaw School of Economics,

University High School in Toruń), but also institutions from far-off rankings, operating in small towns (e.g. Złoty Stok near Częstochowa or Zielona near Żuromin) with limited development opportunities. After the competition, school committees sent the answers sheets of all participants, which were the basis for assessing their knowledge and ranking at the Contest. For research purposes, a random selection of 300 answer sheets was made. At the same time, an assessment of the implementation of educational goals of the project was carried out by participants of the Contest. Such research has been carried out since the IV OPiZ, and this study presents the results of the research carried out within the sixth and seventh editions. The research tool was a questionnaire consisting of 26 questions. Apart from the questions aimed at assessing the educational outcomes, there were also those that provided information about the respondents themselves (class, school, town, family entrepreneurship). Self-prepared questionnaires were sent along with documentation of the first stage of the Contest to schools which were randomly selected. The number of questionnaires for individual schools depended on the number of people taking part in the project and ranged from 1 to 10 pieces. In schools, a random participant completed a questionnaire after completing the competition test. In total, 300 questionnaires were sent in the VII OPiZ, and 285 questionnaires were sent back, and due to the lack of complete answers, in the end, 269 questionnaires were processed. In the case of VII OPiZ, 110 questionnaires were prepared for the study, of which 101 were sent back, and for the above-mentioned reason, ultimately, 98 questionnaires were processed.

3.3 Assessment of the educational outcomes of OPiZ by project participants

The questionnaire research was primarily designed to obtain information about students (Table 3.1) and schools (Table 3.2).

The competition is dominated by men, and this difference is 4% in the sixth edition and 12% in the seventh edition (Table 3.3).

Table 3.2 Gender of students

My gender	VI OPiZ (%)	VII OPiZ (%)
a Woman	48	44
b Man	52	56

Source: Own work based on the conducted research.

Table 3.3 Size of the town/city where the respondent's school operates

My school is located in a town with a population of	VI OPiZ (%)	VII OPiZ (%)
a 5,000	2	4
b 5,000–50,000	12	14
c 50,000–100,000	13	10
d 100,000–200,000	25	26
e over 200,000	**48**	**46**

Source: own work based on the conducted research.

Table 3.4 Number of participations in OPiZ

I enter OPiZ	VI OPiZ (%)	VII OPiZ (%)
a For the first time	**52**	**44**
b For the second time	30	35
c For the third time	16	18
d For the fourth time	2	3

Source: Own work based on the conducted research.

The respondent's schools are located mainly in large cities (over 200,000), and this is almost half of the research sample. One-fourth of the students are from medium-sized cities (100,000–200,000), students from 50,000 to 100,000 and 5,000–50,000 cities are half that size. The representation of the smallest towns (2%–4%) is minimal (Table 3.4).

The competition is dominated by participants taking part in it for the first time (52% and 44%), with one-third of participants taking part in it twice. About one-sixth is competing for the third time, and a minimal group (2%–3%) of students are those of the last years of technical high school who have already entered the competition four times (Table 3.5).

Competing with the best students is the main reason for entering the Contest for a quarter of the sample (25% and 27%). Possibility to improve grades from the Introduction to Business course is at a similar level, which is also true for the results achieved from previous participations in our Contest (18% and 21%) of the respondents. Also, a large part treats participation in OPiZ as a means to get to the university of their dreams (17% and 15%). It is important that good opinions about our project were what encouraged as many as 26% of respondents to participate in the sixth edition and 19% in the seventh edition. There are also those (every fifth participant) who chose the Contest over

Table 3.5 Motives for enter OPiZ

I was encouraged to participate in OPiZ by	First stage (%)	Second stage (%)
a **Opportunity to compete with the best students in the country**	25	**27**
b **Promised good grade from *Introduction to Business* course for my participation**	**26**	24
c Possibility to achieve a better result than in the previous edition	18	21
d Possibility to obtain a student record book of a selected university	17	15
e The topic of this edition	15	7
f **Good opinions about this Contest**	**26**	19
g Taking part in the competition, I am exempt from classes	22	20
h I'm here by chance[4]	8	10

Source: Own work based on the conducted research.

Table 3.6 Attitude of students to the "Introduction to Business" course

Introduction to Business is my **favourite course**	VI OPiZ (%)	VII OPiZ (%)
a Yes	20	23
b **Yes, like some other courses**	**60**	**56**
c Yes, from the moment I started competing in the economic contests	12	12
d No	6	9

Source: Own work based on the conducted research.

participating in classes and a few percent who do not know the reason for entering the OPiZ (Table 3.6).

The participants of the competition are mostly fans of the analysed subject, as every fifth person makes such a declaration and more than a half likes this course as much as other school courses (60% and 56%). It is important that the project contributed to a change of interests, as 12% began to like this subject, thanks to the participation in economic contests (Table 3.7).

More than half of the participants entered the Contest to gain additional economic knowledge (56% and 54%). More than a quarter of the sample is here because of the interest in economic issues

Table 3.7 More general reasons for participation in OPiZ

I'm participating in OPiZ because	VI OPiZ (%)	VII OPiZ (%)
a I am interested in economic issues	26	30
b I'm going to start my own business	16	18
c I want to gain additional knowledge	**56**	**54**
d I want to meet people from other cities	10	12
e I want to win a prize	20	25
f Other reason	8	11

Source: Own work based on the conducted research.

Table 3.8 Preparations for entering OPiZ

Entering VII OPiZ resulted in	First stage (%)	Second stage (%)
a I spend more time studying *Introduction to Business.*	18	20
b I follow economic events more often.	**34**	**38**
c I regularly watch (listen to) economic television (radio) programs.	18	18
d I got to know new sources of economic knowledge.	26	30
e Nothing changed.	10	12

Source: Own work based on the conducted research.

(26% and 30%). Other reasons are awards in the competition (20% and 25%) and the intention to start their own business (16% and 18%), and every tenth wanted to meet people from other cities on this occasion (Table 3.8).

The educational benefits associated with the participation in the project are visible, and it is primarily following current economic events for 34% and 38% of the sample, respectively. Thanks to the Contest, as many as 26% and 30% of respondents got to know new sources of economic knowledge, and every fifth of them watches economic TV programs and a similar number studies *Introduction to Business* more frequently (Table 3.9).

Knowledge necessary in the Contest is acquired mainly by occasionally consulting the recommended sources (32% and 30%) of the students. About one-fifth uses only school courses. Every tenth person attends additional classes at school and the groups of those who work several hours a week, and those who spend their free time preparing

Table 3.9 Preparations for entering OPiZ

To prepare to enter OPiZ, I allocate	VI OPiZ (%)	VII OPiZ (%)
a A few hours a week	12	14
b Free time every day	10	12
c **I occasionally looked at the indicated sources**	**32**	**30**
d I attended additional classes organised at school	8	7
e I limited myself to *Introduction to Business* classes	21	19
f I'm not preparing	22	18

Source: Own work based on the conducted research.

Table 3.10 Evaluation of competition questions

2. The questions in the tests were	VI OPiZ (%)	VII OPiZ (%)
a Easy	8	8
b **Interesting**	**52**	**50**
c Hard	28	32
d Very difficult in part	24	21
e Pretty difficult, but it didn't pose a problem	7	11

Source: Own work based on the conducted research.

for competitions are almost equal. About one-fifth of students does not prepare for the competition (Table 3.10).

Half of the participants considered the competition questions interesting (52% and 50%) and one-third difficult (28% and 32%). Some very difficult questions were noticed by a large group, i.e. 24% and 21% of the sample. Despite the indicated difficulty of the questions, a small part had no problems with them (7% and 11%), and 8% of the respondents assessed the competition test as easy (Table 3.11).

Questions in the area of enterprise management had a clear educational effect because not only did they broaden the knowledge of students (32% and 28%) of the sample but they also prompted almost half of them to widen their knowledge (49% and 45%). Every fourth person found out about their business interests (24% and 22%). A small part does not notice any changes in their economic knowledge after taking part in the Contest (13% and 12%; Table 3.12).

Financial knowledge also improved as approximately one-third of students learned the new financial terms (39% and 32%), and a slightly

Table 3.11 The impact of the test on students' knowledge in the area of organisation management

Questions in the area of business management	VI OPiZ (%)	VII OPiZ (%)
a They expanded my knowledge in this area	32	28
b They prompted me to deepen this knowledge	**49**	**45**
c They confirmed my interests in business	24	22
d They brought nothing to my knowledge of this subject	13	12

Source: Own work based on the conducted research.

Table 3.12 The impact of OPiZ on the level of knowledge of students in the area of finance

Through this contest	VI OPiZ (%)	VII OPiZ (%)
a I got to know new concepts in the field of finance.	**39**	32
b I broadened my knowledge about financial institutions.	28	22
c I have confirmed my knowledge of financial concepts and the functioning of financial institutions.	12	13
d I discovered that I did not know some issues in the field of financial management, which I will try to complete.	38	**41**
e I got to know the "world of finance" a bit, even though it is not an area that interests me.	10	13
f I have not gained any additional knowledge.	9	11

Source: Own work based on the conducted research.

smaller group expanded their knowledge of financial institutions (28% and 22%) of the sample. The competition also showed the participants their unfamiliarity with the issues in this area (38% and 41%). Every tenth got to know the so far uninteresting world of finance, and a similar group confirmed the knowledge of this subject in the competition (12% and 13%). The competition did not affect the financial knowledge of every tenth participant (9% and 11%; Table 3.13).

Table 3.13 The impact of OPiZ on the level of students' knowledge regarding entrepreneurship

Entrepreneurship in the test		*VI OPiZ (%)*	*VII OPiZ (%)*
a	**It broadened my knowledge in this area.**	39	**26**
b	**It encouraged me to take an interest in this area.**	**45**	23
c	It encouraged me to study literature in this area.	12	15
d	It shed new light on her own business.	24	17
e	It confirmed me in my plan to open my own business.	17	11
f	It did not affect my attitude towards business.	19	20

Source: Own work based on the conducted research.

Table 3.14 The impact of OPiZ on the level of students' knowledge of the current economic life

Questions about current economic events encouraged me to		*First stage (%)*	*Second stage (%)*
a	Watch economic television and listen to radio programs	28	26
b	**Browse economic portals on the Internet**	**36**	**43**
c	Listen to experts assessing economic events	16	20
d	Independently analyse and assess changes taking place in the environment of enterprises	24	21
e	There have been no changes in my approach to current economic events	20	18

Source: Own work based on the conducted research.

Similar positive didactic effects were indicated by the respondents on entrepreneurship. A significant part of the student sample expanded their knowledge in this field (39% and 26%), and as many as 45% of the participants of the sixth edition became interested in this subject, while 23% did so in the VII OPiZ. A total of 12% and 15% of students, respectively, were motivated to study literature. The Contest also had an impact on the anticipated economic activity, through a new perspective (24% and 17%) and their confirmation in these choices (17% and 11%). A total of 19% and 20% of the respondents did not notice any influence on the attitude towards business (Table 3.14).

Table 3.15 Changes in the students' approach to learning under the influence of OPiZ

Economic knowledge	VI OPiZ (%)	VII OPiZ (%)
a I will extend it if I qualify to the second/third stage of the competition.	18	19
b I will extend it regardless of the result of the competition.	**49**	**62**
c I will extend it because it has become interesting and is no longer boring.	20	18
d I will not pay much attention to it because my participation in the competition was accidental.	11	10

Source: Own work based on the conducted research.

The subject matter raised in questions concerning current economic events encouraged, above all, to follow economic portals on the Internet (36% and 43%). More than a quarter watches economic television programs (28% and 26%), and almost the same group is willing to independently analyse changes in the organisation's environment (24% and 21%). Almost every fifth respondent is more likely to listen to economic experts (16% and 20%). A similar percentage did not notice any changes in their approach to these issues (20% and 18%; Table 3.15).

Extending economic knowledge is declared by almost half of the students from the sixth edition (49%) and the majority from the seventh edition (62%). Almost a fifth of the sample makes this commitment dependent on the good score in the competition (18% and 19%). A similar group changed their attitude to knowledge as the competition test made it interesting (20% and 18%). One-tenth of the sample describes their participation in the competition as accidental (Table 3.16).

Interesting competition questions were the main argument in the field of expectations, as this was indicated by more than half of the competitors (58% and 54%). The efficient organisation of the competition was also assessed highly with the results of 60% and 52% of responses. Communication with the organiser was good according to 18% and 22% of respondents. Every sixth participant is satisfied with the prizes offered (14% and 15%). The upsides also included the invitation to cooperate in organising the school contest (8% and 16%), and a very small amount of participants said that the project did not meet their expectations (3% and 5%; Table 3.17).

The previously indicated satisfaction with participation in the competition translates into the declaration of participation in the next

Table 3.16 Assessment of meeting participants' expectations regarding the participation in the OPiZ

Participating in the OPiZ met my expectations because	VI OPiZ (%)	VII OPiZ (%)
a **The competition ran very smoothly and according to clear rules.**	**60**	52
b **There were interesting questions.**	58	**54**
c There was good communication with the organiser.	18	22
d Schools were invited to cooperate in the second stage of the competition.	8	16
e Attractive prizes were offered.	14	15
f Participation in the competition did not meet my expectations	3	5

Source: Own work based on the conducted research.

Table 3.17 Declarations regarding students' participation in the next edition of the Contest

I will take part in the next edition of OPiZ	VI OPiZ (%)	II OPiZ (%)
a Very willingly.	**46**	**37**
b I do not know yet.	20	22
c I will wait with the decision for the information about the awards.	7	6
d Unfortunately not, because I am graduating.	16	18
e I will not participate due to the preparation for the final exams.	7	7
f I will not participate.	9	10

Source: Own work based on the conducted research.

edition, and as many as 46% of the sixth and 37% of the seventh edition will do so. Every fifth respondent is not yet decided (20% and 22%), and a small amount claims that it depends on the awards (7% and 6%). A similar group intends to focus on the final exams, so they will not participate (7%). Every tenth decided to refrain from participating in the next edition (9% and 10%; Table 3.18).

The reported interest in economic life was confirmed in further educational plans, as every third person is already determined to study economics (37% and 32%), and additionally, a significant group is considering such studies (18% and 22%). It is important that every tenth participant made sure that the choice of such studies was good (10%). A small percentage will not be economists because they intend to

Table 3.18 Plans to study economy-related majors

I am going to study in the field of economics	VI OPiZ (%)	VII OPiZ (%)
a **Yes, I have made up my mind long ago**	**37**	**32**
b Yes, and participation in the OPiZ confirmed me in this decision	9	10
c Yes, although there were other plans until recently	7	8
d I consider such majors	18	22
e No because I'm going to start a business right after high school graduation	7	8
f No because I am choosing a different field of study	22	20

Source: Own work based on the conducted research.

Table 3.19 Students entrepreneurship self-evaluation

Do you consider yourself an entrepreneurial person	VI OPiZ (%)	VII OPiZ (%)
a **Yes because I always try to implement all my plans, even very ambitious ones.**	**68**	**62**
b No	23	20
c I do not know	9	18

Source: Own work based on the conducted research.

become entrepreneurs immediately after graduating from school and starting their own businesses (7% and 8%). Every fifth respondent will study in a different field (22% and 20%; Table 3.19).

Most participants feel that they have "entrepreneurial souls", and in the sixth edition, it is as much as two-third of the sample, although also in the next edition, it is a high percentage (62%). Every fifth respondent has a different opinion (23% and 20%), and some cannot assess themselves in this context (9% and 18%; Table 3.20).

Over half (54%) of the respondents from the sixth edition say that entrepreneurship can be learned, and the largest group (41%) in the next edition has the same opinion. In addition, many believe that some entrepreneurial qualities can be acquired through teaching and learning (39% and 40%). A small group from the VI OPiZ focuses on inborn features (8%), and this is the opinion of almost every fifth participant of the seventh edition (Table 3.21).

Table 3.20 The origin of entrepreneurial traits according to students

Do you think entrepreneurship (as a feature, skill) can be learned	VI OPiZ (%)	VII OPiZ (%)
a Yes	**54**	**41**
b Some entrepreneurial traits can be acquired in the learning process.	39	40
c No because an entrepreneur must be born one.	8	19

Source: Own work based on the conducted research.

Table 3.21 Students' expectations regarding education in entrepreneurship

20. Entrepreneurship education should (choose one answer)	VI OPiZ (%)	VII OPiZ (%)
a **Mainly serve to shape entrepreneurial traits and attitudes**	**41**	**43**
b Focus mainly on knowledge related to starting a business, assessing market opportunities, project feasibility and financial planning.	36	32
c Be mainly done using a method that "goes beyond knowledge" and "requires practical action".	23	25

Source: Own work based on the conducted research.

Entrepreneurship education should mainly rely on shaping entrepreneurial traits and attitudes (41% and 43%). Fewer are concerned with preparing for the role of an entrepreneur, i.e. equipping him with knowledge that will be helpful in solving everyday and strategic tasks (36% and 32%). A similar approach is shared by those who want to adapt to the practical behaviour and activities that future entrepreneurs will encounter on their business path (23% and 25%; Table 3.22).

Almost half of the respondents are children of entrepreneurs (47%–48%). Their entrepreneurial plans take little account of the continuation of the business created by their parents (11% and 13%). Most of them intend to launch a new business venture according to their own ideas (36% and 27%; Table 3.23).

Children from entrepreneurs' families intend to become entrepreneurs just like their parents. The entrepreneurial path is going to be chosen by as many as 86% of the sample from the sixth edition, slightly less in the next edition, but it is also a very high percentage – 78%

Table 3.22 Entrepreneurial traditions in students' families

Are there entrepreneurial traditions in your family	VI OPiZ (%)	VII OPiZ (%)
a Yes, my parent is the owner (partner) of a business.	47	48
b Yes, and I will continue them as the company's successor.	11	13
c Yes, but I will run another business.	36	27
d No.	**53**	**52**

Source: Own work based on the conducted research.

Table 3.23 Entrepreneurial intentions of respondents from entrepreneurs' families

Are you planning to become an entrepreneur	VI OPiZ (%)	VII OPiZ (%)
a Yes, after graduating from high school	17	18
b Yes, after graduating from university	**53**	**36**
c Yes, in an undefined future	10	16
d No, I prefer to be a well-paid employee	14	22
e I do not know yet	6	8

Source: Own work based on the conducted research.

(the sum of items excluding point d). Slightly more than half of them want to gain the necessary knowledge in advance through economic studies (53%), and one-third of the VII OPiZ (36%) have a similar plan. A surprisingly large group does not want to wait to start a business and intends to do so right after graduating from high school (17% and 18%). Slightly fewer people have not decided when to start their own business (10% and 16%). Employee status is chosen by a small percentage of participants in the sixth edition (14%) and every fifth participant in the VII OPiZ (22%). A small number do not yet know the answer to the question about the professional future (6% and 8%).

The assessment of the educational effects of the project by the participants should be considered high. The organisational side is positively assessed, but most of all also the substantive side of the Contest is. Both the participants of the VI and VII OPiZ described the competition questions as difficult, but interesting, and this applies to all distinguished areas of economic knowledge. In each case, it is claimed that additional knowledge is gained, thanks to the project in the form of learning new economic concepts, knowledge about financial institutions or economic life. Participation in the project discovered the lack of knowledge and ignorance regarding many issues that the students intend to learn more about. Good score in the competition, i.e. promotion to the next stage, is an additional motivator, and interestingly, for some participants, thanks to the Contest, economic knowledge became more interesting or even changed from boring to interesting. The confirmation of the attractiveness of the project for most participants is the declaration of participation in the next edition. It is important that the educational outcomes, i.e. the benefits of participating in the Contest increase with the level of the competition, as exemplified by the analysis of the results of research carried out for second and third stages of the contest. Students with good scores spend more time studying (Table 3.24).

With every stage, the commitment of students increases. Already in the second stage of the competition, 40% consult the indicated sources, and the share of those who spend several hours a day preparing for the competition or use their free time to study increases slightly (by 6% and 2%). Attendance at additional school classes increases minimally (by 1%). Number of those who do not study for the contest drops by 8%. There are clear changes in the preparations among the finalists. Almost half (48%) work several hours a week, and every fifth (22%) studies at the expense of their free time. More than 4% of students, compared to the second stage of the competition, take part in additional classes and all prepare for the competition decisive for winning the Contest.

Table 3.24 Preparation of students for I, II and III stages of the VII OPiZ

To prepare myself for the VII OPiZ, I spent	First stage (%)	Second stage (%)	Third stage (%)
a **A few hours a week**	12	18	**48**
b Free time every day	10	12	22
c **I occasionally looked at the indicated sources**	**32**	**43**	23
d I attended additional classes organized at school	8	9	13
e I limited myself to *Introduction to Business* classes	21	14	0
f I'm not preparing	22	18	0

Source: Own work based on the conducted research.

Table 3.25 Changes in students' attitudes to economic knowledge depending on the stage of the VII OPiZ

Economic knowledge	First stage (%)	Second stage (%)	Third stage (%)
a I will extend it if I qualify to the second/third stage of the Competition.	18	19	–
b **I will extend it regardless of the result of the competition.**	**49**	**62**	**79**
c I will extend it because it has become interesting and is no longer boring.	20	15	17
d I will not pay much attention to it because my participation in the competition was accidental.	11	8	0

Source: Own work based on the conducted research.

The attitude to economic knowledge changes positively with the increasing stage of the contest (Table 3.25).

The declaration of interest in economic knowledge increases significantly, and the group that will expand this knowledge regardless of the result of the competition is growing by 13% in the second round. Among the finalists, this percentage is as high as 79%. Similar declarations were registered in individual areas of knowledge, confirming the increased interest in economic sciences and studies at such universities, but also a greater share of people interested in their own business or intending to concentrate their professional life around business, also as managers.

3.4 Analysis of students' economic knowledge

To study the economic knowledge of students, participants of the first stage of the VI OPiZ, a questionnaire was prepared, also acting as a competition test in the project, consisting of 50 closed-ended questions, each of which contained four answers, where only one was correct [Appendix 1]. Due to the competitiveness, the test was limited to 60 minutes. The questions were to reveal the economic knowledge of students from its particular areas, i.e. entrepreneurship, the functioning of the enterprise, its environment, micro and macroeconomics. Questions in the area of finance were also prepared from the level of the household, enterprise, to the problems of the state budget and the capital market. The growing turbulence of the environment, with its unforeseen events, such as the coronavirus pandemic, referred to as *Black Swans*,[5] made it necessary to prepare a few questions checking the tracking of current economic events. To show knowledge in specific areas, questions were divided into ten thematic blocks. The number of questions in individual blocks varies and ranges from three to eight questions, which was related to the complexity of a given block, but also to the implementation of other goals beyond research, i.e. the educational goal and the nature of the competition. Also, the level of difficulty of the questions varies, so the smaller number of difficult questions seems to give a similar view of the knowledge of the respondents as the larger number of the easier ones. The questionnaire is dominated by questions about the environment not only about its variability and increasing impact on operating enterprises but also practice shows, in the authors' opinion, that the "new" entrepreneurs who are just starting are focused primarily on the venture and the offered product (service) and pay less attention to what is happening outside the organisation. Of course, the market with its most important entities, i.e. the client and competitors is followed by them, while the general environment is monitored and analysed to a lesser extent. Importantly, the changes taking place here, especially in the legal situation in our country, require their ongoing monitoring. New regulations introduced in recent years affect the functioning of enterprises, regardless of their size or type of business. These undoubtedly include changes in the labour law, with their growing (minimum) wages or with regard to forms of employment and that is why issues related to this subject have a separate block. A similar approach was used in relation to other areas, and the resulting thematic blocks were:

1 *Entrepreneurship* (PRZED)
2 *Business management* (ZP)
3 *Enterprise finance management* (ZFP)
4 *General environment – economic conditions* (OO_UE)
5 *General environment – Legal conditions – Commercial Companies Code* (UP_KSH)
6 *General environment – Legal conditions – labour law and the labour market* (UP_PPiRP)
7 *Capital investments* (IK)
8 *Economy* (EK)
9 *General economic knowledge* (OWE)
10 *Current economic events* (BWG)

The questions and the scores of correct answers given by students in individual blocks are presented below. Correct answers are shown in bold.

1   *Entrepreneurship* (PRZED), seen here in the narrow sense, as a process of setting up a business enterprise, consists of five questions.

1 Entrepreneur according to R.W. Griffin is a person who	Correct answers
a Organises a business	78.7%
b Runs a business	
c Takes the risk associated with the business	
d Meets all the above-mentioned conditions	
2 In order to start a company, an entrepreneur must have at his disposal share capital in an amount of not less than	Correct answers
a PLN 5,000	51.3%
b EUR 5,000	
c PLN 50,000	
d EUR 50,000	
3 An entrepreneur who is also a full-time employee is obliged to pay insurance contributions on his own	Correct answers
a sickness insurance	30.3%
b pension insurance	
c accident insurance	
d health insurance	
4 Among the social insurance contributions paid by the entrepreneur, which is the non-compulsory insurance contribution?	Correct answers
a sickness insurance	31.3%
b disability pension	
c accident insurance	
d health insurance	
5 Which statement about big American entrepreneurs is not true?	Correct answers
a Jeff Bezos is the founder of Amazon.	34.3%
b Mark E. Zuckerberg is a co-founder of Facebook.	
c John D. Rockefeller, co-founder of Standard Oil, is considered the richest man in history.	
d Warren Buffett is the founder of the US retail chain called Wal-Mart.	

2 *Business management* (ZP) was tested using five questions.

1 The diversification strategy consisting in expanding the offer by proposing new products, often completely unrelated to those produced so far, for new types of customers is	Correct answers
a horizontal diversification	
b conglomerate diversification	**48.0%**
c concentric diversification	
d none of the above	
2 Which statement regarding *Kanban* is not true?	Correct answers
a This is one of the most famous production innovations of the Toyota Corporation.	
b This is a method commonly known as *Kaizen*.	**53.3%**
c This method is based on individual product cards, their circulation and analysis.	
d The essence of this method is to strive to eliminate all inventory from the production process.	
3 Products (businesses in a corporation) that have a small share in the rapidly growing market are, according to the method of analysing the company's products, called *BCG matrix*	Correct answers
a milk cows	
b stars	**28.3%**
c dogs	
d question marks	
4. Increasing the scope of the bicycle producer's operational activity by purchasing a company that is a tire supplier is	Correct answers
a centralisation	
b diversification	**27.7%**
c total horizontal integration	
d total vertical integration	
5 *Hidden champions* in Polish conditions are companies that	Correct answers
a Occupy first, second or third places on the European market and are leaders on the Polish market.	
b Have revenues below EUR 3 billion.	**43.7%**
c Are not settled in the public consciousness (anonymity).	
d Meet all the above-mentioned conditions.	

3   *Corporate financial management* (ZFP) consists of six questions.

1	Financing the company's operations with retained profit means financing	Correct answers
	a own external	
	b borrowed external	
	c own internal	69.7%
	d borrowed internal	
2	An entrepreneur using factoring as a seller of receivables before the date of their collection is defined as	Correct answers
	a debtor	
	b factor	
	c factoree	83.3%
	d none of the above	
3	Current assets are not	Correct answers
	a inventory	
	b means of transport	
	c short-term investments	32.0%
	d short-term prepayments	
4	We calculate the receivables turnover ratio as	Correct answers
	a total current assets ÷ total current liabilities	
	b total current liabilities ÷ total current assets	
	c total current assets ÷ current liabilities	18.3%
	d liquid current assets ÷ current liabilities	
5	An entrepreneur who is a VAT payer pays to the tax office	Correct answers
	a Input VAT	
	b Output VAT	
	c the difference of input and output VAT	22.3%
	d the difference between output and input VAT	
6	The amount of tax paid by the entrepreneur in the form of a fixed amount tax does not depend on	Correct answers
	a type of business	
	b the number of employees employed	
	c the number of inhabitants of the commune in which the activity is conducted	27.7%
	d period of activity	

4 *General environment – economic conditions* (OO_UE) is a block represented by five questions.

1 The EUR area includes	Correct answers
a Serbia	
b Sweden	68.0%
c Slovakia	
d Switzerland	
2 The Free Trade Agreement between the EU and Canada, which entered into force on September 21, 2017 is	Correct answers
a CETA	
b FTA	46.7%
c NAFTA	
d TTiP	
3 According to Eurostat data on the public sector deficit in the EU countries in 2016, the least indebted country in terms of GDP is	Correct answers
a Estonia	
b Germany	36.3%
c Poland	
d Sweden	
4 State policy aiming to protect the domesticmarket from competing with imported goods is defined as	Correct answers
a deontology	
b physiocracy	54.0%
c monetarism	
d protectionism	
5 The nominal value of GDP in 2016 amounted to	Correct answers
a approx. PLN 1.55 trillion	
b approx. PLN 1.85 trillion	40.3%
c approx. USD 1.1 trillion	
d approx. EUR 1.1 trillion	

5 *General environment – Legal conditions – Commercial Companies
   Code* (UP_KSH) is a block where knowledge was tested using four
   questions.

1	The supervisory board of a joint-stock company listed on the Stock Exchange is appointed by	Correct answers
	a Management Board	
	b The President of the Warsaw Stock Exchange	**22.3%**
	c The Minister of Treasury	
	d General Meeting of Shareholders	
2	The supervisory board should be established	Correct answers
	a in each limited joint-stock partnership	
	b in each limited liability company	**69.7%**
	c in each joint-stock company	
	d in each of the above-mentioned businesses	
3	A partnership is not	Correct answers
	a private partnership	
	b professional partnership	**63%**
	c limited partnership	
	d limited joint-stock partnership	
4	Which statement regarding general partnership is not true?	Correct answers
	a General partnership is established upon entry in the register of entrepreneurs.	
	b General partnership agreement should be concluded in the form of a notarial deed.	
	c The business name of a general partnership should contain the names or business names of all partners or the name or business name of one or more partners.	**37.7%**
	d Each partner is obliged to run the partnership's affairs, for which he does not receive remuneration.	

6 General environment – *Legal conditions – labour law and the labour market* (UW_PPiRP) are covered in four questions.

1 An entrepreneur employing a student under a mandate agreement is obliged to pay him an hourly rate of at least		Correct answers
	a PLN 12 gross	63%
	b PLN 12 net	
	c PLN 13 gross	
	d PLN 13 net	
2 According to the estimates of the Central Statistical Office, the number of employees receiving remuneration in the amount of the minimum wage is		Correct answers
	a about 0.4 million people, 8%	25.3%
	b about 1.4 million people	
	c about 2.4 million people	
	d about 3.4 million people	
3 The unemployment rate in September 2017 decreased to the level of		Correct answers
	a 10.8%	59.3%
	b 8.8%	
	c 6.8%	
	d 4.8%	
4 The total cost of employing an employee for the minimum wage (2017) on the side of the employer is		Correct answers
	a PLN 2,012.20	73.7%
	b PLN 2,212.20	
	c PLN 2,412.20	
	d PLN 2,612.20	

7 *Capital Investments* (IK), as broad knowledge of the capital market with trading financial instruments (shares, futures, options) on the stock exchange and currency trading (Forex) consists of seven questions.

1 The most expensive currency as of 31 October 2017 was	Correct answers
a CZK	
b CHF	
c EUR	**75.7%**
d GBP	
2 A share is	Correct answers
a derivative	
b debt security	
c equity security	**83.3%**
d all of the above	
3 The stock market EPS indicator informs about	Correct answers
a What is the profit per share?	
b How many times is the company's value on the market greater (smaller) than its book value?	
c How many times does the company's market value exceed the value of the profit earned during the year?	**52.0%**
d How many times is the highest share price higher (lower) than the share issue price?	
4 The interest rate after eliminating the effects of inflation and taking into account taxation is	Correct answers
a nominal interest rate	
b real interest rate	
c effective interest rate	**40.7%**
d discount rate	
5 The Monetary Policy Council at its last meeting (November 2017)	Correct answers
a Lowered interest rates	
b Left interest rates unchanged	
c Raised interest rates	**52.3%**
d None of the above answers is true	

6 The exclusive right to issue the currency of the Republic of Poland is vested in	Correct answers
a The Minister of Finance	77.7%
b The National Bank of Poland	
c Warsaw Stock Exchange	
d State Securities Printing House (PWPW SA)	
7 An investor who wants to sell shares quickly, regardless of the price, and who does not want to risk that the order will be partially executed, should place an order	Correct answers
a PKC	44.3%
b PCR	
c PCRO	
d Stop loss	

8 *Economy* (EK) is knowledge of micro and macroeconomics, checked through three questions.

1 A producer's market is when	Correct answers
a The supply of a given good or service is greater than the demand.	46.7%
b The demand for a good or service is greater than the supply.	
c The offered goods or services are produced exclusively by domestic producers.	
d The market is a monopsony.	
2 The shift in the butter demand curve cannot be caused by	Correct answers
a decrease in the price of butter	63.0%
b increase in the price of margarine	
c increase in nominal income of the population	
d a change in consumers' tastes regarding butter	
3 If the propensity to save increases, then	Correct answers
a Work efficiency declines	44.3%
b Investments decrease	
c The number of technical devices increases	
d Capital consumption increases	

9 *General economic knowledge* (OWE) understood here as practical economic knowledge that every human being should have in their professional and private lives, which, due to its wide scope, consists of seven questions.

1 On a PLN 100 note there is a portrait of	Correct answers
a Fryderyk Chopin	
b Adam Mickiewicz	
c King Władysław II Jagiełło	**99.0%**[6]
d Maria Skłodowska-Curie	
2 Damaged banknote which has 45%–75% of its original size, will be exchanged	Correct answers
a for half of its nominal value	
b for 75% of its nominal value	**34.0%**
c for its full nominal value	
d will not be exchanged	
3 The author of *The wealth of nations* is	Correct answers
a P.F. Drucker	
b I.M. Kirzner	**53.3%**
c A. Smith	
d J.A. Schumpeter	
4 Which statement about special economic zones (SEZ) is not true?	Correct answers
a SEZs are administratively distinguished areas of the country, where entrepreneurs may conduct business activity, obtaining regional aid in the form of exemption from (part of) income tax.	
b The purpose of the SEZ operation is to accelerate the development of regions through, among others, attracting new investments, developing export and creating new workplaces.	**32.0%**
c The required minimum investment value in SEZ is EUR 100,000.	
d There are currently 24 SEZ in operation.	

5 Municipal property is otherwise one that is	Correct answers
a municipal	
b state	
c private	66.0%
d capital company	
6 Richard H. Thaler received the Nobel Prize in Economics 2017 for	Correct answers
a analysis of consumption, poverty and welfare	
b developing a theory on the merger of cartels and regulations affecting the activities of monopolists	
c achievements in the field of consumption analysis, monetary history and theory, and presenting the complexity of the stabilisation policy	43.7%
d scientific contribution to the development of behavioural economics	
7 The oldest currency in the world that is over 1,200 years old and still in circulation is	Correct answers
a U.S. dollar	
b Australian dollar	
c British pound	66.0%
d Swiss franc	

10   *Current economic events* (BWG) consist of four questions.

1 Vistula and Bytom are well-known Polish brands from the industry of	Correct answers
a household appliances	
b electronic devices	
c clothing items	81.7%
d food products	
2 The city called the capital of Polish copper is	Correct answers
a Katowice	
b Sosnowiec	
c Jastrzębie-Zdrój	51.3%
d Lubin	
3 Which e-commerce estimates are not true?[7]	Correct answers
a The number of online stores exceeds 35,000.	
b Estimated e-commerce market value is approx. PLN 40 billion.	
c In 2020, the value of the e-commerce market may reach PLN 63 billion.	10.4%
d Already in 2014, a statistical Pole made purchases on the Internet for an amount exceeding EUR 500.	
4 According to the *Forbes* magazine's ranking, the largest Polish private company is	Correct answers
a CCC	
b Ciech	
c Cyfrowy Polsat	51.3%
d LPP	

Source: Own work.

The assessment of students' knowledge in individual areas began with the use of descriptive statistics. The obtained results were presented for two types of results, e.g. for point scales (according to the scores obtained by participants) and for standard scales. The dimension scales were constructed in such a way that the value 0 was assigned to students who did not have any correct answer and the value 1 to those having all correct answers. The result was therefore a comparison of the scale values for individual dimensions. In the case of point scales,

Table 3.26 Descriptive statistics for the point dimension scales of research questions

Topic area	N	Mean	Std. dev.	Std. error of the mean	Min.	Q25	Median	Q75	Max.
PRZED	300	2.28	1.17	0.07	0.0	1.0	2.0	3.0	5.0
ZP	300	1.98	1.34	0.08	0.0	1.0	2.0	3.0	5.0
ZFP	300	2.53	1.35	0.08	0.0	2.0	2.0	3.0	6.0
OO_UE	300	2.85	1.29	0.07	0.0	3.0	4.0	5.0	7.0
UP_KSH	300	1.35	1.04	0.06	0.0	1.0	1.0	2.0	4.0
UP_PPiRP	300	2.02	1.12	0.06	0.0	1.0	2.0	3.0	4.0
IK	300	4.03	1.51	0.09	0.0	3.0	4.0	5.0	7.0
EK	300	1.87	0.81	0.05	0.0	1.0	2.0	2.0	3.0
OWE	300	3.77	1.34	0.08	0.0	3.0	4.0	5.0	7.0
BWG	300	1.97	0.97	0.06	0.0	1.0	2.0	3.0	4.0

Source: Own work based on A. Brzeziński, *Kompetencje w zarządzaniu wspolczesną organizacją*, Wydawnictwo Politechniki Częstochowskiej, Częstochowa 2019, p. 134.

the areas are incomparable because they consist of a different number of questions, so standard scales ranging from 0 to 1 were used for level comparisons. Descriptive statistics for point scales are presented in Table 3.26.

The posted results show that, for the questions in the *Entrepreneurship* (PRZED), block students got on average 2.28 points. The standard deviation here is 1.17, which proves that the results of individual students deviate from the average value by ±1.17 points. This measure shows the diversity between students. The greater its value, the greater the diversity and the greater the difficulty for the participants. The standard error of the mean for this block is 0.07, so the mean is 2.28 points ±0.07. The minimum number of points that students receive in this area is 0. At least 25% of students received one point or less, at least 50% received two points or less and at least 75% of students received three points. The maximum number of points received is five, i.e. if all the answers were correct.

In the *Business management* (ZP) block, the average was lower and amounted to 1.98 points. The standard deviation was 1.34, which proves that the results of individual students deviate from the average value by ±1.34 points. The standard error of the mean for this area is 0.08. The obtained mean is 1.98 points ±0.08. The minimum number of points received by the respondents is 0. At least 25% of students received one point or less, at least 50% received two points or less and at least 75% of students received three points. The maximum number of points received is five, i.e. if all the answers were correct.

In the case of the *Enterprise finance management* (ZFP), block students obtained an average of 2.53 points. The standard deviation was 1.35, showing that the results of individual students deviated from the average value by ±1.35 points. With a standard error value of 0.08, the mean is 2.53 points ±0.08. The minimum number of points obtained by the respondents in this block is 0. At least 25% of students received two point or less, at least 50% received two points or less and at least 75% of students received three points. The maximum number of points obtained is six.

In the *General environment – economic conditions* (OO_UE) block, the students' average score was 2.85 points. The standard deviation is 1.29, so the results of individual students deviate from the average by ±1.29 points. The standard error of the mean for this block is 0.07, so the mean is 2.85 points ±0.07. The minimum number of points received by the respondents is 0. At least 25% of the students received a maximum of two points, at least 50% received a maximum of three points and at least 75% of the students received four points. The maximum score is five points.

In the *General environment – Legal conditions – Commercial Companies Code* (UP_KSH) block, the respondents obtained an average of 1.35 points. With a standard deviation of 1.04, so the results of individual students deviate from the mean by ±1.04 points. Since the standard error was 0.06, the mean is 1.35 points ±0.06. The minimum number of points received by the respondents in this area is 0. At least 25% of students received one point or less, at least 50% received one point or less, at least 75% of students received two points and the maximum number of points was four.

In the last block related to *General Environment – Legal conditions – labour law and the labour market* (UP_PPiRP), the students received an average of 2.02 points. The standard deviation for this area is 1.12, which proves that the results of individual students deviate from the average value by ±1.12 points. The standard error of the mean is 0.06, so the mean is 2.02 points ±0.06. The minimum number of points received by students in this block is 0. At least 25% of students received one point or less, and at least 50% received two points or less. At least 75% of the students received three points, and the maximum score was four points.

In the financial block called *Capital investments* (IK), the average students' score was 4.03 points, which is the best result among all the subject areas. The standard deviation for this area is 1.51, so individual students' results deviate from the average by ±1.51 points. This value is also the highest among all analysed areas. It should therefore be emphasised that there is the greatest diversity between the examined students and the greatest difficulty in this area. The standard error is 0.09, so the mean is 1.51 points ±0.09. The minimum number of points received by the respondents is 0. At least 25% of students received a maximum of three points, at least 50% received a maximum of four points, at least 75% of students received five points and the maximum number was seven.

In the *Economy* (EK) block, the students' average score was 1.87 points. The standard deviation is 0.81, which proves that the results of individual students deviate from the average value by ±0.81 points. This value is the lowest among all subject areas, which means that, in this case, we have the smallest diversity between the examined students, and therefore, the lowest difficulty in this area. The standard error of the mean is 0.05, resulting in an average of 1.87 points ±0.05. The minimum number of points received by the respondents in the EK area is 0. At least 25% of students received one point or less, at least 50% received two points or less, at least 75% of students received two points and the maximum number of points was three.

In the block called *General Economic Knowledge* (OWE), the average students' score was 3.77 points. The standard deviation for this area is 1.34, which shows that the results of individual students deviate from the average by ±1.34 points. With a standard error value of 0.08, the mean is 3.77 points ±0.08. The minimum number of points received by the respondents in the area of OWE is 0. At least 25% of students received three points or less, at least 50% received four points or less and at least 75% of students received five points. The maximum score was seven points.

In the last block called *Current economic events* (BWG), the average student score was 1.97 points. The standard deviation has the value of 0.97, which proves that the results of individual students deviate from the average value by ±0.97 points. The standard error of the mean is 0.06, so the mean is 1.97 points ±0.06. The minimum number of points received by the respondents in the BWzZG area is 0. At least 25% of students received one point or less, at least 50% received two points or less and at least 75% of students received three points. The maximum number of points received is four.

It should be emphasised in the summary that the highest average number of points received by students occurred in the block called *Capital investments* IK (4.03), while the lowest one was in the General Environment – UP_KSH block (1.35).

Descriptive statistics for normalised scales are shown in Table 3.27.

Table 3.27 Descriptive statistics for standardised dimension scales of questions testing students' knowledge

Subject area	N	Mean	Std. dev.	Std. error of the mean	Min.	Q25	Median	Q75	Max.
PRZED	300	0.46	0.23	0.01	0.0	0.20	0.40	0.60	1.0
ZP	300	0.40	0.27	0.02	0.0	0.20	0.33	0.50	1.0
ZFP	300	0.42	0.23	0.01	0.0	0.33	0.33	0.50	1.0
OO_UE	300	0.57	0.26	0.01	0.0	0.40	0.60	0.80	1.0
UP_KSH	300	0.34	0.26	0.02	0.0	0.25	0.25	0.50	1.0
UP_PPiRP	300	0.51	0.28	0.02	0.0	0.25	0.50	0.75	1.0
IK	300	0.58	0.22	0.01	0.0	0.43	0.57	0.71	1.0
EK	300	0.62	0.27	0.02	0.0	0.33	0.67	0.67	1.0
OWE	300	0.54	0.19	0.01	0.0	0.43	0.57	0.71	1.0
BWG	300	0.49	0.24	0.01	0.0	0.25	0.50	0.75	1.0

Source: Own work based on A. Brzeziński, *Kompetencje ...* op. cit., p. 137.

The presented results can be treated as a percentage (%) of the correct answers. In the *Entrepreneurship* (PRZED) block, on average, 46% of correct answers were given, and in the field of Business Management (ZP), it was 40%. *Enterprise finance management* (ZFP) had an average result of 42%, and a much higher percentage – 57% was observed in the block called *General environment – economic conditions* (OO_UE). A low score of correct answers, 34%, was observed in the area of *General environment – Legal conditions – Commercial Companies Code* (UP_KSH). In the next block on the General Environment (UP_PPiRP), this result slightly exceeds half (51%), and in the block called *Capital investments* (IK), average result is 58%. Economics Questions (EK) had the best score of 62%. In the last blocks, i.e. General Economic Knowledge (OWE), an average of 54% was observed, and in the Current Economic Events (BWG) block, it was 49%. Legal conditions – labour law and the labour market (UP_PPiRP) – 51%.

The comparison of the results shows that the best results were obtained by the students in the blocks: *Economics, Capital Investments, General Environment – economic conditions,* the worst results were obtained in the block: *Legal conditions – Commercial Companies Code.* The greatest diversity of results was recorded in the following areas: *Legal conditions – labour law and the labour market, Business management, Economics,* the lowest diversity: *General Economic Knowledge.*

Note that, in the case of the block called *Legal conditions – Commercial Companies Code,* the median was only 0.25, i.e. at least 50% of the students obtained a poor result of only 25% correct answers. A similarly low result (33%) is observed for the block called *Enterprise finance management*. For these subject areas, there is also the greatest difference between the mean and the median, which proves the asymmetry of the answers. Since the mean is greater than the median, it should be stated that most of the students answered poorly (below the average), and only a small percentage of students correctly answered most of the questions. The developed histograms of answers to the questions for individual subject blocks are presented in Figures 3.1–3.10.

Figure 3.1 shows that the largest group (almost 90) in the PRZED block are students who answered two questions correctly. There are also almost equal groups (70 people each) who answered one and three questions correctly, respectively. Almost 40 students answered four questions, and about ten people answered all five questions and just over ten respondents did not answer any question in this area correctly.

In this block, two equal groups (almost 80 people each) gave one or two correct answers. Over 60 students gave three correct answers and over 40 gave no correct answer. A group of 30 students scored four points, and the maximum number of five points was achieved by slightly more than ten students.

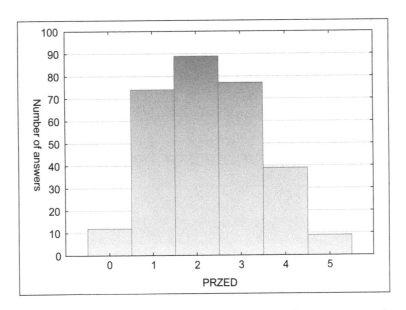

Figure 3.1 Histogram of answers to questions in the *Entrepreneurship* (PRZED) block.

Source: Own work based on A. Brzeziński, *Kompetencje...* op.cit., p. 138.

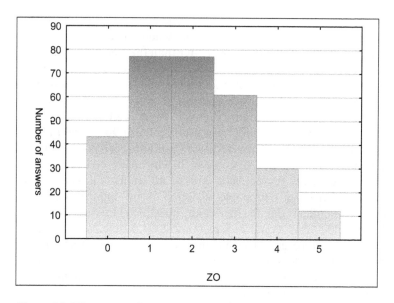

Figure 3.2 Histogram of answers to questions in the area of *Business management* (ZP).

Source: Own work based on A. Brzeziński, *Kompetencje...*op.cit., p. 140.

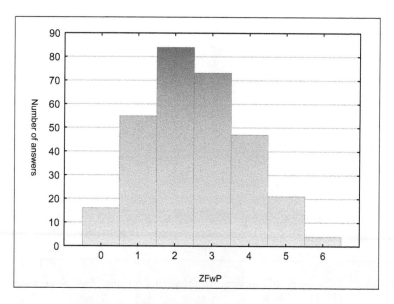

Figure 3.3 Histogram of answers to questions from the *Enterprise finance management* (ZFP) block.

Source: Own work based on A. Brzeziński, Kompetencje... op.cit., p. 140.

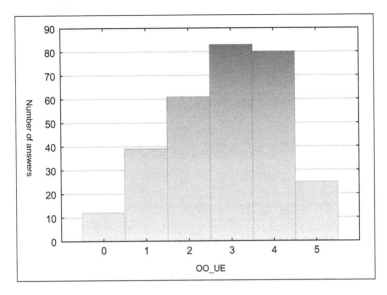

Figure 3.4 Histogram of answers to questions in the *General environment –*
economic conditions (OO_UE) block.
Source: Own work based on A. Brzeziński, *Kompetencje...op.cit.*, p. 143.

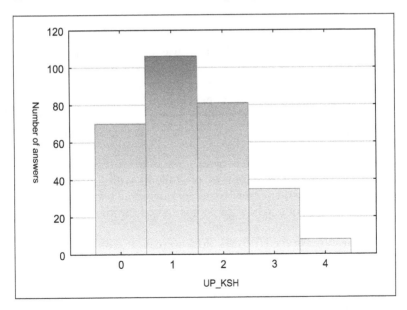

Figure 3.5 Histogram of answers to questions in the *General environment –*
Legal conditions – Commercial Companies Code (UP-KSH) block.
Source: Own work based on A. Brzeziński, *Kompetencje...op.cit.*, p. 142.

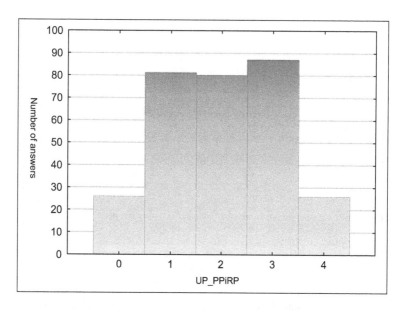

Figure 3.6 Histogram of answers to questions in the *General environment –
Legal conditions – labour law and the labour market* (UP_PPiRP)
block.

Source: Own work based on A.Brzeziński, *Kompetencje...*op.cit., p. 139.

In the ZFP block, greater diversity was observed, and the largest
group (over 80 people) are students who correctly answered two questions. Over 70 students scored three points and approx. 55 people
scored one point. Slightly less than 50 respondents scored four points,
and we have about 20 students with as many as five correct answers. A
few of the respondents scored the maximum number of points (6), and
unfortunately, a dozen or so people got zero points.

The largest group (over 80 people) are students with a result of three
points (OO_UE), and the number of students with four correct answers is slightly smaller. Over 60 students answered two and almost 40
people – one question. About 25 people scored the maximum number
of points and over ten scored zero.

The questions in the UP-KSH block were clearly difficult for about
70 people (0 points), and over 100 students answered one question correctly. Two points were scored by 80 students, three – by almost 40,
and only a few students scored all four points.

More than 25 people (four answers) did great in the legal block (UP_
PPiRP), but a similar group did not answer any question correctly.
Almost 90 people gave correct answers to three questions and about
80 to two and one question.

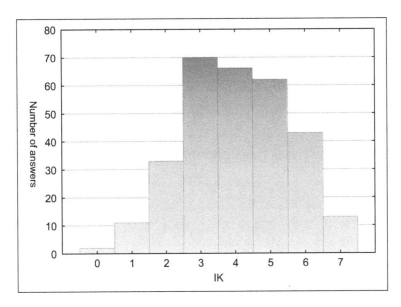

Figure 3.7 Histogram of answers to questions in the area of *Capital invest-ments* (IK).
Source: Own work based on A. Brzeziński, *Kompetencje*...op.cit., p. 141.

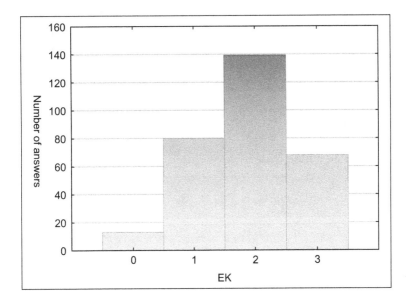

Figure 3.8 Histogram of answers to questions in the area of *Economy* (EK).
Source: Own work based on A. Brzeziński, Kompetencje...op.cit., p. 142.

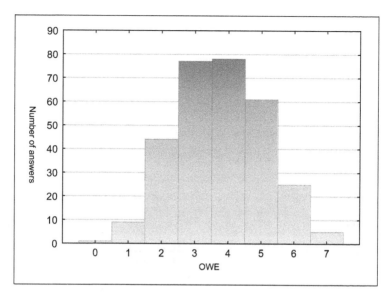

Figure 3.9 Histogram of answers to questions in the area of *General economic knowledge* (OWE).

Source: Own work based on A. Brzeziński, *Kompetencje*...op.cit., p. 144.

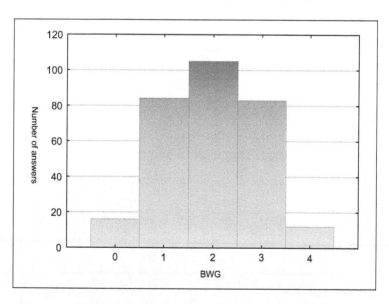

Figure 3.10 Histogram of answers to questions in the area of *Current economic events* (BWG).

Source: Own work based on A. Brzeziński, *Kompetencje*...op.cit., p. 142.

In the financial block called *Capital investments* (Figure 3.5), i.e. the issues that were "closest" to the students' interests and which, importantly, was the block with a large number of questions, there is a group of 70 people with two points. A little fewer students have three and a little over 60 scored five. Quite a few students (over 40) got six points, and over ten people had all the correct answers (seven). Almost the same number had one and very few because only two to three people in this block scored zero.

The largest group (almost 140 people) scored two points, and almost 80 students scored one point. Almost 70 people scored three points (max). For over ten people, the economic questions were a complete surprise (0 points).

In the block with the most questions, almost 80 answered four and slightly fewer three questions correctly. Over 60 students scored five points, 25 as many as six and approximately five got maximum score (seven points). Lower marks, i.e. two points, were scored by approx. 45 people, almost ten students scored one point and probably a single student did not score any point.

Questions about *Current economic events* (BWG) were a complete surprise for almost 20 people, but more than ten had a maximum score. Over 100 students scored two points, and about 80 people scored one and a similar number scored three.

Summarising the histogram analysis, it can be stated that:

- in case of blocks: PRZED, EK, BWG and OWE, a typical distribution was observed for the answers
- a uniform distribution was identified in the UP_PPIRP block, i.e. students responded almost evenly
- in the field of ZFP, an asymmetry of answers was observed, which proves that more students responded below the average, and five or six points were scored by relatively few students who overstated the average
- asymmetry was identified in the ZP block, but smaller than in the previous case of ZFP
- in the case of IK, most students answered correctly, and only a small group scored 0 or 1 point, and this group, in turn, lowered the mean (although the asymmetry here is also lower than in the case of ZFP)
- in the UP_KSH block, the asymmetry of the answers was observed – more students scored below the average, five or six points were scored by relatively few students, which translates into overstating the average

- in the area of OO_UE, most of the students answered correctly, and only a small group scored 0 or 1 point, and they underestimate the mean (this asymmetry, however, is lower than in the case of ZFP)

The obtained results showed that the students' economic knowledge is at a different level in the individual subject blocks that have been distinguished here for analysis. Among the subject blocks, the students have the highest knowledge in the *Economy* (EK) and *Capital investments* (IK) blocks. The high mean of correct answers in economics (EK) at a level of 62% shows good knowledge of the issues in this area, and the average below the median (67%) proves that this is the score of the majority of students. Another interesting result is IK, where more than seven questions were used. Questions in this area concerned the functioning of an investor on the stock exchange and the conditions affecting (favouring or not) this type of investments. The questions were not only beyond the scope of compulsory school education programme in the theoretical part but could also indicate practical knowledge of a capital market investor. This is confirmed by specific questions about stock exchange orders, which are rather known to stock exchange users. The low value of the standard deviation (0.22) shows that it is a significant percentage of the respondents. Practical functioning on the capital market means that they have already taken risks, which is particularly related to this type of activity. Moreover, it is an activity with a high degree of risk for the owner of the capital, so the entrepreneurial plans declared in the previously analysed surveys could be undertaken with full awareness of these risks.

A good result was also noted in the area of knowledge, which, according to the authors, is important in entrepreneurial activities, i.e. knowledge about the company's environment. The block concerning the general environment, i.e. the layer of the environment that is beyond the influence of market participants, has been allocated to the economic conditions sector (OO_UE). The positive trends occurring here have a positive influence on the growth and development, especially when it comes to beginning entrepreneurs. There were five questions on this subject, for which the arithmetic mean of correct answers was 57%, and it was below the median of 60%. This proves that more than half of the students observe and perhaps analyse the ongoing economic processes. The result in the *General economic knowledge* (OWE) category is also satisfactory. This area includes knowledge of economic issues and terms, which is useful not only in the professional life of every employee, but also in private life, it is necessary to know specific economic rules and laws in order to profitably manage the household budget. The scope of such knowledge is quite wide and varied, so there were as many as seven questions in this area. The knowledge of the issues required here was met with an average of correct answers at the level of 54% and also with a lower value than the median (60%). It should be noted that the lowest answer variation in comparison to other areas was noted here, as the value of the standard deviation was only 0.19. Also, in this area, there was a question that was answered correctly by as many as 99% of students.

Slightly more than half of the correct answers (51%) were observed in the case of the area also related to the general environment, i.e. *Legal conditions – labour law and the labour market* (UP_PPiRP). Knowledge of this area and the requirement of constant observation due to the volatility of regulations are also necessary for every employer, manager and employee. The picture of this knowledge is slightly spoiled by the fact that the mean value is lower than the median (0.50). A similar result (0.49) was observed for students following current economic events (BWG). It is an equally important property that allows you to update the knowledge about the environment and the opportunities and threats to the functioning of the organisation that appear there. Almost half of the students are aware of this. Entrepreneurship (PRZED) scores were poorer. Questions relating to the start-up of business ventures, related requirements and the entrepreneur himself got an average score on a level of 0.46. Unfortunately, this value clearly exceeds the median (0.40), so the result was determined by the correct answers of the minority of good students, with poor results of the majority of the sample. Knowledge in the field of organisation has been divided into the area of business management (ZP) and enterprise financial management (ZFP). Knowledge of financial resources management, where questions related to the topics of the financial ratio, balance sheet or tax obligations, was slightly wider with a score of 0.42. However, this area is familiar to the minority of the sample, as the median is clearly lower than the mean (0.33). In this respect, the issues of organisation management (equal mean and median) look better, where knowledge of strategic management instruments or organisational structures was aligned with the scores at the level of 40%. Even though the score is not high, equal median and the arithmetic mean are somewhat comforting. The worst score is related to the knowledge regarding legal regulations for the functioning of an enterprise. Mostly, regulations relating to the start-up and operation of enterprises, i.e. the *Legal conditions – the Commercial Companies*

Code (UP_KSH) block. Questions related mainly to businesses (capital and personal) revealed gaps in this area, as the worst score was recorded here, with the average score at the level of 0.34. Unfortunately, it was primarily the knowledge of the best students in the sample, as the median was only 0.25, and it was this group that overstated the already poor result.

3.5 Summary of research results

Developing the results of empirical research carried out among participants of the first stage of the VI Entrepreneurship and Management Contest (OPiZ) was the achievement of empirical goals and the answer to the research questions posed. A picture of the level of students' knowledge of management and entrepreneurship in the area of the organisation and its environment was obtained. Detailed analysis of the research material showed, inter alia, that the students:

a   Consider themselves (mostly) entrepreneurial and half of them intend to become entrepreneurs; some just after graduating from school.
b   Are partially planning a managerial career, which, combined with an earlier declaration, means that their professional life will be associated with enterprises.
c   Half of them are children of entrepreneurs.
d   Most of them plan to continue their education at economic universities.

These results highlight the importance of school education in the field of entrepreneurship and management. According to the respondents, this education should focus primarily on creating entrepreneurial attitudes and behaviours and then on transferring knowledge. It also seems to be understandable because, in the Internet age, access to many sources of information is very easy.

The tested students' level of knowledge in the field of entrepreneurship and management revealed diversified knowledge of issues in individual subject blocks and gave the following results:

•   Students showed the highest level of knowledge in the field of capital investments and economics. Practical knowledge was also noted in the first area, which showed that some of the respondents had experience on the Stock Exchange. Male students were a majority, which may indicate that, already at this age, this gender is more prone to taking actions with higher risk, and investments in the capital market are risky. Questions about economics were purely theoretical, so the good score obtained here may indicate that theoretical knowledge that dominates in school education (and actually not only here) is also easier to assimilate by students.

- Knowledge of the issues in the block on economic conditions in general environment was also good, which is a good signal for business planners, as the entrepreneurial experience of the authors shows that beginning entrepreneurs focus primarily on the offered product and the functioning of the company being launched. The environment of the organisation is analysed here only in the layer of the closer (competitive) environment, while general environment and its individual sectors are monitored with little attention.
- A slightly poorer result was observed in the case of the general environment and the sector of legal conditions in the field of labour law.
- General knowledge of economics gave comforting results because apart from professional life, it is more and more needed in private life in managing the household budget or properly responding to offers made by various financial institutions.
- Entrepreneurship and business management were ranked further downstream. In terms of managing a business, good knowledge of strategic management instruments and much worse knowledge of starting a business were noted.
- The worst score was observed for legal knowledge in the area of the *Commercial Companies Code* although it should be noted here that the volatility of economic law in the last years gives little chance for students to keep up with it, as entrepreneurs also struggle with it.

Notes

1 The list of winners is available in the *OPiZ winners* tab on the website of the Contest: https://olimpiada.wz.pcz.pl/zwyciezcy-opiz-VIII2019 [accessed May 20, 2020].

2 See http://licea.perspektywy.pl/2020/tabele/ranking-glowny-liceow [accessed May 20, 2020].

3 The Częstochowski Olimpijczyk is a regional competition involving schools from Częstochowa, and the former Częstochowa Province, as well as two nearby cities, Wieluń and Radomsko, students from there have been taking part in the Contest from the first edition.

4 Although participation in the Contest is voluntary, some students may be enrolled by teachers to obtain a good result in the competition of schools in the "Entrepreneurial school" category, where success is determined by the number of participants in the project.

5 *The Black Swan* is a term introduced by NN Taleb describing extreme, unpredictable events, the occurrence of which has very negative consequences: NN Taleb, *The Black Swan*, Ed. Zysk i spółka, Poznań 2020.

6 This is the best result in this study and even in the history of the Contest.

7 This question was the most difficult for the students. Only every tenth respondent knew the correct answer.

Summary

The research we conducted in this monograph allowed for a positive verification of the following research hypothesis:

> Economic education of Polish youth cannot be left in the hands of family and household, but it must be institutional and international, and it should be coordinated and controlled by state bodies using standard and non-standard instruments.

As a result of the research, the necessity of acquiring economic knowledge, especially macroeconomic knowledge, by young people who set up households early, take over companies from their parents, make decisions – first group decisions with their parents at home – then independently in their own household, was unequivocally justified. The modern world throws various information at young people: facts, cases, examples on social media, on television, in the press, Facebook, LinkedIn, Messenger, on the radio, and it seems that we managed to show in this monograph *how to connect these various sources of economic knowledge with the effects of research into economic theory in this area.*

In the monograph, we stated that economic education in Poland should combat the following stereotypes that young people in the West have been familiar with for at least 100 years.

Stereotype 1: Risk aversion and failure disrespect culture

The American ethos of an entrepreneur for whom failure is normal in running a business. The more failures an entrepreneur has, the more often he is considered to be more ambitious and courageous.

Observing Polish and foreign entrepreneurs, it is very difficult to find those for whom business failure is an expression of enormous ambition and courage. The environment cannot separate their financial failure from the personal qualities of such people. We still too rarely learn from the failures of others, but we underestimate those entrepreneurs who want to build a professional business, even though they have not successfully completed their first project.

Stereotype 2: No second chance culture

Recovering from a business failure is extremely difficult and painful in Europe. Entrepreneurs must show exceptional resilience and fight the pressure imposed by the environment. In the USA, it is believed that any business that is opened after previous failure has a greater chance of success.

Stereotype 3: Lack of self-confidence

Compared to the Americans, we still have too little faith in our own abilities. We can laugh at the attitude of "grinning with their beautiful white smiles" New Yorkers or residents of Texas, but note that, from an early age, they have been learning the attitude of "Yes, I can".

Stereotype 4: Self-employment is a risk, we are too conservative

Although the number of self-employed people (micro-entrepreneurs) already exceeds 3 million, as one of the previous texts wrote, most of these enterprises are simply companies established to provide services to one or two clients. Few people are brave enough to take the risk and build bigger businesses. The fear of failure is so strong that Polish entrepreneurs are afraid that if they fail, they may even have a problem with going back to full-time employment. Because they will be considered failures. And if so, it's better not to start at all.

Stereotype 5: Lack of economic education and unstable law

Young Poles often think that:

a   entrepreneurship cannot be learned

b the law must change because the environment of economic processes is turbulent.

General conclusion that results from our research described in this monograph:
   Entrepreneurship can be learned by following these rules:

a first of all, we shall explain to young people precisely what entrepreneurship is
b then the rules on how to become an entrepreneur should be presented
c finally, we shall show how to be an entrepreneur
d entrepreneurship can be learned using standard instruments, that is, by studying in various types of schools, taking postgraduate training courses, as by using non-standard instruments, that is, by active work in school business incubators or participation in entrepreneurship and management Contests.

It seems that, in this way, we have fulfilled all our intentions which prompted us to write this monograph because we have positively verified the research hypothesis and achieved the main goal of the monograph.

References

Acs, Z.J., Szerb, L., Autio, E. (2015), Enhancing Entrepreneurship Ecosystems. A "Systems of Entrepreneurship" Approach to Entrepreneurship Policy. In: *Global Entrepreneurship and Development Index 2015*. Springer Briefs in Economics. Springer, Cham. https://doi.org/10.1007/978-3-319-26730-2_4

Święcka, B. (2008), *Bankructwa gospodarstw domowych. Perspektywa ekonomiczna i społeczna*, Difin, Warszawa.

Aronson, E. (2009), *Człowiek istota społeczna*, PWN, Warszawa, Wyd. 12.

Blaug, M. (2000), *Teoria ekonomii. Ujęcie retrospektyczne*, Polskie Wydawnictwo Naukowe PWN, Warszawa.

Bochenek, M. (2002), *Początki ekonomii akademickiej w Europie, "Ruch prawniczy, dzekonomiczny i socjologiczny"*, Rok LXIV, zeszyt 1, Poznań.

Brzeziński, A. (2016), *Przedsiębiorczość. Teoria i praktyka*, Wydawnictwo Wydziału Zarządzania Politechniki Częstochowskiej, Częstochowa.

Brzeziński, A. (2018), *Wiedza ekonomiczna. Testy i zadania*, Wydanie drugie. Wydawnictwo Wydziału Zarządzania Politechniki Częstochowskiej, Częstochowa.

Brzeziński, A. (2019), *Kompetencje w zarządzaniu współczesną organizacją*, Wydawnictwo Politechniki Częstochowskiej, Częstochowa.

Damasio, A. (2013), *Błąd Kartezjusza. Emocje, rozum i ludzkość*, Wyd. II Rebis, Poznań.

Daze, S., Sharma, M., Lalandle, L., Riahi, S. (2009), *Draft Chart of Available Entrepreurship Support in Ottawa*, Ottawa, Ontario, Canada 21 October.

Europejski Dom Spotkań – Fundacja Nowy Staw, ETÖK, Union Haddiema Maghqudin (UHM) (2016), *Model Inkubatora Przedsiębiorczości dla szkół zawodowych*, Erasmus+, Lublin.

Flis, I., Makiewicz, M. (2010), *Własna firma*, Wydawnictwo Naukowe PWN, Warszawa–Bielsko-Biała.

Goszczyńska, M., Kołodziej, S., Trzcińska, A. (2012), *Uwikłanie w świat pieniądza i konsumpcji. O socjalizacji ekonomicznej dzieci i młodzieży*, Difin, Warszawa.

Krzyżanowski, L.J. (1999), *O podstawach kierowania organizacji inaczej*, PWN, Warszawa.

Landreth, H., Colander, D.C. (1998), *Historia myśli ekonomicznej*, PWN, Warszawa.

Landreth, H., Colander, D.C. (2002), *History of Economic Thought*, 4th ed., Houghton, Mifflin, Florida USA.

Lange, O. (1959), *Ekonomia polityczna*, t. I, *Zagadnienia ogólne*, PWN, wyd. drugie, Warszawa.

Lavelle, J., Matusiak, K.B., Krukowski, K., Mażewska, M., Zasiadły, K. (1997), *Inkubator Przedsiębiorczości*, MPiPS, MBOiR, Warszawa.

Lipiec, I., Nizioł, P., Łątka (2016), *Model inkubatora przedsiębiorczości dla szkół zawodowych w Polsce, [w:]*, Wydawnictwo: Europejski Dom Spotkań – Fundacja Nowy Staw, ETOK, UHM, *Model inkubatora przedsiębiorczości dla szkół zawodowych*, Lublin.

Majewski, B. (2011), *Świadomość i dojrzałość ekonomiczna nastolatków – wyniki badania w roku szkolnym 2010/2011*, e-mentor nr 1(38) 2011, Wydawnictwo SGH Warszawa.

Multan, E.,Walczuk, K., *Rola_inkubatorow_akademickich_w_rozwoju_przedsiębiorczosci_w_Polsce*. Pdf – dostęp; accessed 13/07/2020.

NBP (2019), *Diagnoza stanu wiedzy i świadomości ekonomicznej dzieci i młodzieży w Polsce*, Departament Edukacji i Wydawnictw NBP, 16 maja, Warszawa.

Noga, B., Noga, M. (2019), *Zarządzanie ryzykiem w procesie podejmowania decyzji ekonomicznych przez organizacje*, CEDEWU, Warszawa.

Noga, B., Noga, M., Dejnaka, A. (2019), *Edukacja ekonomiczna polskiego społeczeństwa*, CEDEWU, Warszawa.

Noga, M. (2009), *Makroekonomia*, Wyd. Akademii Ekonomicznej we Wrocławiu, Wrocław.

Noga, M. (2014), *Kultura a ekonomia*, CEDEWU.PL, Warszawa.

Noga, M. (2017), *Neuroekonomia a ekonomia głównego nurtu*, CEDEWU, Warszawa.

Pikuła-Małachowska, J. (2016), *Akademickie Inkubatory Przedsiębiorczości – szansa dla młodych przedsiębiorców*, "Marketing i Zarządzanie", nr 4, *MSP - z doświadczeń województwa pomorskiego i Elbląga*, "Gospodarka lokalna i regionalna w teorii i praktyce", nr 46.

QAA (2012), *Enterprise and Entrepreneurship Education. Guidance for UK Higher Education Providers, Draft for Consultations*, The Quality Assurance Agency for Higher Education, February 2012, Mimeo.

Riahi, S. (2010), *Youth Entrepreneurship:Ottawa's Portfolio in Talent Development*, Technology Innovation Management Review [TIM], November.

Robbins, L. (1932), *An Essay on the Nature and Significance of Economic Science*, Mc Millan, London.

Samuelson, P., Nordhaus, W.D. (1998), *Ekonomia 1*, Wydawnictwo Naukowe PWN, Warszawa.

Samuelson, P., Nordhaus, W.D. (2010), *Economics*, 19th ed., McGraw – Hill/ Irwin, NY USA.

Sedláček, T. (2012), *Ekonomia dobra i zła. W poszukiwaniu istoty ekonomii od Gilgamesza do Walk Street*, Wyd. Studio Emka, Warszawa.

Sikora, J. (2011), *Edukacja ekonomiczna jako ważny składnik kształcenia przedzawodowego*, Wyd. Wyższa Szkoła Pedagogiczna TWP, Warszawa.

Stankiewicz, W. (2007), *Historia myśli ekonomicznej*, PWE, Warszawa.

Szewczuk, W. (2000), *Podstawy psychologii*, Warszawa Wyd. Fundacja Innowacja.

Sztompka, P. (2002), *Socjologia. Analiza społeczeństwa*, Wyd. Znak, Kraków.

Tyszka, T. (2010), Decyzje. *Perspektywa psychologiczna i ekonomiczna*, Scholar, Warszawa.

Wach, K. (2013), *Edukacja na rzecz przedsiębiorczości wobec współczesnych wyzwań cywilizacyjno-gospodarczych*, Wyd. Uniwersytetu Ekonomicznego w Krakowie "Przedsiębiorczość- Edukacja", nr 9.

Websites

http://kellog.campusgroups.com/isc/h
http://columbiasocialenterprise.org
http://www.hbs.edu/socialenterprise/businessplan
http://globalchallenge.mit.edu
http://www.weforum.org
http://www.universitynetwork.org
https://timreview.ca/article/394
https://charaktery.eu/artykul/naturalna-swiadomosc; accessed 18/05/2020
https://encyklopedia.pwn.pl/haslo/myslenie;4009251; accessed 20/05/2020
https://eur-lex.europa.eu> TXT> PDF; accessed 29/05/2020
https://eur-lex.europa/legal-content/PL/TXT/?uri=LEGISSUMI%3Axy0026; accessed 29/05/2020
https://eurydice.org.pl; accessed 29/05/2020
https://www.szkolnafirma.pl; accessed on 20/04/2020
https://gimversity.pl; accessed 29/05/2020
https://instytutobywatelski.pl, AK Koźmiński, Economic perceptions of Poles, Civic Institute, Warsaw February 4, 2014; accessed 04/12/2015
https://junior.org.pl; accessed 29/05/2020
https://Klp.pl/mitologia/a-7272.html; accessed 19/05/2020
https://kognitywistyka.net; accessed 18/05/2020
http://licea.perspektywy.pl/2020/tabele/ranking-glowny-liceow
https://m.xelion.pl> gielda; accessed 25/05/2020
https://www.szkolnafirma.pl; accessed 10/05/2020
https://www.szkolnafirma.pl; accessed 30/04/2020
https://ore.edu.pl; accessed 29/05/2020
https://poland.us/strona, 5,895,0,edukacja-w-usa-szkoly...; accessed 29/02/2020
https://sip.lex.pl/akty-prawne/dzienniki-UE/rewolucja-parlamentu...; accessed 29/05/2020
https://uniwersytet-dzieciecy.pl; accessed 29/05/2020
https://Klp.pl/mitologia/a-7272.html; accessed 19/05/2020
https://www.coig.com.pl/Baza_szkol_w_Polsce.php, accessed 29.05.2020

https://www.money.pl/gospodarka/wiadomosci/artykul/wiedza-o-f,   dostęp; accessed 29/05/2020

http://s.inkubatory.pl/pl/sie_aip; accessed 16/05/2014

https://www.szkolnafirma.pl; accessed 13/07/2020

http://www.pi.gov.pl/parp/chapter_96055.asp?soid=0EBBEEB340F14D 10BEC5982F5031C232; accessed 16/05/2014

http://biznesflow.pl/czym-jest-startup/; accessed 17/05/2016

https://cwrkdiz-konin.pl/szkolne-inkubatory-przedsiebiorczosci/accessed 12/07/2020

http://www.inkubatory.pl; accessed 16/05/2014

mfiles.pl> index.php> swadomosc...; accessed 18/05/2020

https://sip.lux.pl/akty-prawne/dzienniki-UE/rezolucja-parlamentu...; accessed 29/05/2020

www.olimpiada.wz.pcz.pl; accessed: 20/06/2020

https://biznesnaostro.pl/przedsiebiorczosc- w-usa-d Why-taka-p...; accessed 29/05/2020

http://www.e-mentor.edu.pl/artykul/index/numer/34/id/730; accessed 29/05/2020

www.nbp.portal.pl; accessed 29/05/2020

mfiles.pl> index.php> incubator_przed Przedsiębiorczości/ accessed 08/07/2020

www.uniwesytet-dzieciecy.pl; www.gimversity.pl; accessed 29/05/2020

Annex no. 1

A set of questions that was used to test the students' economic knowledge.

1 Entrepreneur according to R.W. Griffin is a person who
  a   organises a business
  b   runs a business
  c   takes the risk associated with the business
  d   meets all the above-mentioned conditions

2 In order to start a company, an entrepreneur must have at his disposal share capital in an amount of not less than
  a   PLN 5,000
  b   EUR 5,000
  c   PLN 50,000
  d   EUR 50,000

3 Vistula and Bytom are well-known Polish brands from the industry of
  a   household appliances
  b   electronic devices
  c   clothing items
  d   food products

4 An entrepreneur employing a student under a mandate agreement is obliged to pay him an hourly rate of at least
  a   PLN 12 gross
  b   PLN 12 net
  c   PLN 13 gross
  d   PLN 13 net

5 The city called the capital of Polish copper is
  a   Katowice
  b   Sosnowiec
  c   Jastrzębie-Zdrój
  d. Lubin

6 The euro area includes
   a   Serbia
   b   Sweden
   c   Slovakia
   d   Switzerland

7 The most expensive currency as of October 31, 2017 was
   a   CZK
   b   CHF
   c   EUR
   d   GBP

8 An entrepreneur who is also a full-time employee is obliged to pay insurance contributions on his own
   a   sickness insurance
   b   pension insurance
   c   accident insurance
   d   health insurance

9 Among the social insurance contributions paid by the entrepreneur, which is the non-compulsory insurance contribution?
   a   sickness insurance
   b   disability pension
   c   accident
   d   health insurance

10 An entrepreneur who is a VAT payer pays to the tax office
   a   input VAT
   b   output VAT
   c   the difference of input and output VAT
   d   the difference between output and input VAT

11 Financing the company's operations with retained profit means financing
   a   own external
   b   borrowed external
   c   own internal
   d   borrowed internal

12 The amount of tax paid by the entrepreneur in the form of a fixed amount tax does not depend on
   a   type of business
   b   the number of employees employed
   c   the number of inhabitants of the commune in which the activity is conducted
   d   period of activity

13 The supervisory board of a joint-stock company listed on the Stock Exchange is appointed by
   a   Management Board
   b   The President of the Warsaw Stock Exchange
   c   The Minister of Treasury
   d   General Meeting of Shareholders

14 The supervisory board should be established
   a   in each limited joint-stock partnership
   b   in each limited liability company
   c   in each joint-stock company
   d   in each of the above-mentioned businesses

15 A share is
   a   a derivative
   b   debt paper
   c   share paper
   d   each of the above

16 A partnership is not
   a   private partnership
   b   professional partnership
   c   general partnership
   d   limited joint-stock partnership

17 Which statement regarding general partnership is not true?
   a   General partnership is established upon entry in the register of entrepreneurs.
   b   General partnership agreement should be concluded in the form of a notarial deed.
   c   The business name of a general partnership should contain the names or business names of all partners or the name or business name of one or more partners.
   d   Each partner is obliged to run the partnership's affairs, for which he does not receive remuneration.

18 An entrepreneur using factoring as a seller of receivables before the date of their collection is defined as
   a   debtor
   b   factor
   c   factoree
   d   none of the above

19 The Free Trade Agreement between the EU and Canada, which entered into force on September 21, 2017, is
   a   CETA
   b   FTA

    c   NAFTA

    d   TTIP

20 A producer's market is when

    a   The supply of a given good or service is greater than the demand.

    b   The demand for a good or service is greater than the supply.

    c   The offered goods or services are produced exclusively by domestic producers.

    d   The market is a monopsony.

21 Which statement about special economic zones (SEZs) is not true?

    a   SEZs are administratively distinguished areas of the country, where entrepreneurs may conduct business activity, obtaining regional aid in the form of exemption from (part of) income tax.

    b   The purpose of the SEZ operation is to accelerate the development of regions through, among others, attracting new investments, developing export and creating new workplaces.

    c   The required minimum investment value in SEZ is EUR 100,000.

    d   There are currently 24 SEZs in operation.

22 The shift in the butter demand curve cannot be caused

    a   decrease in the price of butter

    b   increase in the price of margarine

    c   increase in nominal income of the population

    d   a change in consumers' tastes regarding butter

23 If the propensity to save increases, then

    a   work efficiency declines

    b   investments decrease

    c   the number of technical devices increases

    d   capital consumption increases

24 Current assets are not

    a   inventory

    b   means of transport

    c   short-term investments

    d   short-term prepayments

25 The interest rate after eliminating the effects of inflation and taking into account taxation is

    a   nominal interest rate

    b   real interest rate

    c   effective interest rate

    d   discount rate

26 The total cost of employing an employee for the minimum wage
    (2017) on the side of the employer is
    a   PLN 2,012.20
    b   PLN 2,212.20
    c   PLN 2,412.20
    d   PLN 2,612.20

27 The stock market EPS indicator informs about
    a   What is the profit per share?
    b   How many times is the company's value on the market greater
         (smaller) than its book value?
    c   How many times does the company's market value exceed the
         value of the profit earned during the year?
    d   How many times is the highest share price higher (lower) than
         the share issue price?

28 We calculate the receivables turnover ratio as
    a   total current assets ÷ total current liabilities
    b   total current liabilities ÷ total current assets
    c   total current assets ÷ current liabilities
    d   liquid current assets ÷ current liabilities

29 The diversification strategy consisting in expanding the offer by
    proposing new products, often completely unrelated to those pro-
    duced so far, for new types of customers is
    a   horizontal diversification
    b   conglomerate diversification
    c   concentric diversification
    d   none of the above

30 Which statement regarding *Kanban* is not true?
    a   This is one of the most famous production innovations of the
         Toyota Corporation
    b   This is a method commonly known as *Kaizen*
    c   This method is based on individual product cards, their circu-
         lation and analysis
    d   The essence of this method is to strive to eliminate all inven-
         tory from the production process

31 Products (businesses in a corporation) that have a small share in
    the rapidly growing market are, according to the method of ana-
    lysing the company's products, called *BCG matrix*
    a   milk cows
    b   stars
    c   dogs
    d   question marks

32 Increasing the scope of the bicycle producer's operational activity by purchasing a company that is a tire supplier is
   a   centralisation
   b   divergence
   c   total horizontal integration
   d   total vertical integration

33 *Hidden champions* in Polish conditions are companies that
   a   occupy first, second or third places on the European market and are leaders on the Polish market
   b   have revenues below EUR 3 billion
   c   are not settled in the public consciousness (anonymity)
   d   meet all the above-mentioned conditions

34 Which statement about big American entrepreneurs is not true?
   a   Jeff Bezos is the founder of Amazon.
   b   Mark E. Zuckerberg is a co-founder of Facebook.
   c   John D. Rockefeller, co-founder of Standard Oil, is considered the richest man in history.
   d   Warren Buffett is the founder of the US retail chain called Wal-Mart.

35 The Monetary Policy Council at its last meeting (November 2017)
   a   lowered interest rates
   b   left interest rates unchanged
   c   raised interest rates
   d   none of the above answers is true

36 Which e-commerce estimates are not true?
   a   The number of online stores exceeds 35,000.
   b   Estimated e-commerce market value is approx. PLN 40 billion.
   c   In 2020, the value of the e-commerce market may reach PLN 63 billion.
   d   Already in 2014, a statistical Pole made purchases on the Internet for an amount exceeding EUR 500.

37 According to Eurostat data on the public sector deficit in the EU countries in 2016, the least indebted country in terms of GDP is
   a   Estonia
   b   Germany
   c   Poland
   d   Sweden

38 The unemployment rate in September 2017 decreased to the level of
   a   10.8%
   b   8.8%

c   6.8%

d   4.8%

39 According to the *Forbes* magazine's ranking, the largest Polish private company is

a   CCC

b   Ciech

c   Cyfrowy Polsat

d   LPP

40 Municipal property is otherwise one that is

a   municipal

b   state

c   private

d   capital company

41 Richard H. Thaler received the 2017 Nobel Prize in Economics for

a   analysis of consumption, poverty and welfare

b   developing a theory on the merger of cartels and regulations affecting the activities of monopolists

c   achievements in the field of consumption analysis, monetary history and theory, and presenting the complexity of the stabilisation policy

d   scientific contribution to the development of behavioural economics

42 State policy aiming to protect the domestic market from competing with imported goods, is defined as

a   deontology

b   physiocracy

c   monetarism

d   protectionism

43 There is a portrait on the PLN 100 note of

a   Fryderyk Chopin

b   Adam Mickiewicz

c   King Władysław II Jagiełło

d   Maria Skłodowska-Curie

44 The oldest currency in the world that is over 1,200 years old and still in circulation is

a   US dollar

b   Australian dollar

c   British pound

d   Swiss franc

45 Damaged banknote, which has 45%–75% of its original size, will be exchanged

a   for half of its nominal value

b   for 75% of its nominal value

c   for its full nominal value

d   will not be exchanged

46 The exclusive right to issue the currency of the Republic of Poland is vested in

a   The Minister of Finance

b   The National Bank of Poland

c   Warsaw Stock Exchange

d   State Securities Printing House (PWPW SA)

47 An investor who wants to sell shares quickly, regardless of the price, and who does not want to risk that the order will be partially executed, should place an order

a   PKC

b   PCR

c   PCRO

d   Stop Loss

48 According to the estimates of the Central Statistical Office, the number of employees receiving remuneration in the amount of the minimum wage is

a   about 0.4 million people

b   about 1.4 million people

c   about 2.4 million people

d   about 3.4 million people

49 The nominal value of GDP in 2016 amounted to

a   approx. PLN 1.55 trillion

b   approx. PLN 1.85 trillion

c   approx. USD 1.1 trillion

d   approx. EUR 1.1 trillion

50 The author of *The wealth of nations* is

a   P.F. Drucker

b   I.M. Kirzner

c   A. Smith

d   J.A. Schumpeter

Index

Note: **Bold** page numbers refer to tables; *italic* page numbers refer to figures and page numbers followed by "n" denote endnotes.

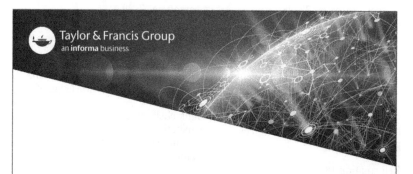

Taylor & Francis eBooks

www.taylorfrancis.com

A single destination for eBooks from Taylor & Francis
with increased functionality and an improved user
experience to meet the needs of our customers.

90,000+ eBooks of award-winning academic content in
Humanities, Social Science, Science, Technology, Engineering,
and Medical written by a global network of editors and authors.

TAYLOR & FRANCIS EBOOKS OFFERS:

A streamlined
experience for
our library
customers

A single point
of discovery
for all of our
eBook content

Improved
search and
discovery of
content at both
book and
chapter level

REQUEST A FREE TRIAL
support@taylorfrancis.com

 Routledge
Taylor & Francis Group

 CRC Press
Taylor & Francis Group